"A GATEWAY TO THE 21ST CENTURY OF MEDICINE"

THE RESTORATION OF THE

HUMAN

BODY

[IN 7 PARTS]

RESTORE YOUR BODY - OPTIMIZE YOUR HEALTH

SERGEY A. DZUGAN, MD, PHD
KONSTANTINE S. DZUGAN

The Restoration of the Human Body in Seven Parts

ISBN: 978-0-9885802-0-6

Printed in the United States of America

This book is dedicated to my family: my wife Yelena and three sons Sergey, Alexander, and Konstantine.

Table of Contents

Foreword

Peter G. Fedor-Freybergh, MD, PhD, Dr.h.c. mult.
Obstetrician, Gynecologist, Child Psychiatrist,
Psychiatrist, Psychotherapist

Jenny Beatriz Loria Muñoz, MD
Director of Aesthetic Services

Professor George Birkmayer MD PhD
Professor of Medicine and Medical director

----

*Peter G. Fedor-Freybergh, MD,
PhD, Dr.h.c multi.
Obstetrician, Gynecologist,
Psychiatrist, Child Psychiatrist,
Psychotherapist*

"We stay on the intellectual shoulders
of the giants of medicine from past days
and we are able to see further than they did
only because they helped us to do so."
Claude Bernard

"Imagination is more important than knowledge"
Albert Einstein

The new book by Dr. Sergey Dzugan that you hold in your hands "The Restoration of the Human Body" is an excellent, most unique masterpiece - a gateway to the 21st century of medicine. The book is written in an easy-going way, like a pirouette by a prima ballerina seemingly so light and easy, but yet demanding of highest professionalism, training and thorough knowledge of each detail involved... It is an elegant piece of work of high scientific level and at the same time understandable in common sense, even amusing, written both for professionals and laymen alike - a book for the intelligent reader. This book is a must and should be possessed by libraries, university libraries, and bookshelves of private persons, even as a bedside pleasure.

I am proud and happy that I was bestowed with the honor of writing a foreword to this book. I remember meeting Dr. Dzugan for the first time at the International Anti-Aging congress in Milan. After his brilliant lecture the overwhelmed audience rushed out to get his signature on his previous book "Your Blood Doesn't Lie", which was a fascinating reading for me as well.

Sergey Dzugan's book discusses at length the science behind physiologic decline and how it can be restored, about the art of aging, presenting enough information in the best way possible so that the reader can have a better understanding of how our bodies work. A question is posed in 'How does the restoration of human physiology work?' Sergey Dzugan's answer is 'by natural approach, which takes into account a multitude of subsystems that need to be fixed so that the body is rejuvenated to what we enjoyed in our 20s'.

One of the quotes to this foreword is by Claude Bernard, who beside of being a great physiologist of all time has also seen the close connections between science and art. Claude Bernard believed that the artist can find more stable grounds in science and that the scientist may generate a safe intuition from art. He was convinced that if physiology progressed long enough, there would be an understanding between the poet, the philosopher and the physiologist.

The human life should be considered as an indivisible continuum where each of the developmental stages is equally important, all stages interdependent and inseparable from the whole individual's life continuum. In this continuum, the individual represents the indivisible entity of all functions on physiological or physical, psychological and social levels. The physical, biochemical, endocrinological, immunological and psychological processes represent a whole which cannot be divided.

The transdisciplinary and integrative aspect of sciences and their entree in 21st century is the true vision for our common efforts - in this light I also see this new book by Sergey Dzugan. Reading it gave me much pleasure and inspiration and I warmly recommend it to the broad public of both professionals and interested laymen.

I wish this book a successful journey!

****

Peter G. Fedor-Freybergh is Obstetrician, Gynecologist, Psychiatrist, Child Psychiatrist, Psychotherapist;
Professor in Psychoneuroendocrinology, Child and Adolescent Psychiatry;
Professor in Prenatal and Perinatal Psychology and Medicine;
Editor-in-Chief of NEUROENDOCRINOLOGY LETTERS
Co-Editor in Chief of BIOGENIC AMINES
Founder and Editor-in-Chief of INT J OF PRENATAL & PERINATAL PSYCHOLOGY & MEDICINE
Co-Chief Editor of ACTIVITAS NERVOSA SUPERIOR REDIVIVA
Honorary Life President: International Society of Prenatal and Perinatal Psychology and Medicine

Jenny Beatriz Loria Muñoz, MD.
Medical Director
Med Spa de Cancun, Mexico

It has been a pleasure to have met Dr. Dzugan and much more of an honor to be one of the people to give a foreword. As a medical doctor I have been exposed to general, aesthetic and "anti–aging" medicine, but the knowledge that I have achieved by experimenting with this horizon through the eyes of Dr. Dzugan, for me has been "the missing link" - that has joined all my previous studies, investigations, and days of hard work. I think this book is an opportunity for anyone who really wants to learn and understand the human body and its physiology.

For me the human body is like a puzzle, that now makes more sense and thanks to Dr. Dzugan's guidelines (which he so kindly chooses to share,) I feel more secure and confident that now I'm "really preventing and healing" which was always my goal when I was a very young woman and chose this profession. My recommendation to everyone, especially my colleagues, is to read this book and unlock the door to your new horizon.

It is logical! It is Physiology! It is The Restoration of the Human Body!

****

Jenny Beatriz Loria Munos is the Medical Director of Wellness and Cosmetic Laser Center Med Spa de Cancun, Mexico

Professor George Birkmayer, MD PhD

This book is exciting in many senses. It provides a lot of very valuable information for health conscious people. Dr. Dzugan describes difficult physiological processes in simple terms by using comparisons to actions in our daily life. For me, most importantly he sweeps away certain dogmas of mainstearm medicine e.g. that lowering cholesterol will improve your health. All his arguments are based on solid scientific evidence.

In Part I *"On the History of Medicine and the Nature of Disease,"* Dr. Dzugan points out that "medicine has roots deep in prehistory." For me it was interesting to learn that even animals are eating certain plants for their health problems. What Egyptian, Persian and Greek healers were able to accomplish with their methods in their patients and what impact this had on modern medicine is described in a most entertaining way.

In Part II *"On the Pitfalls of Conventional Medicine,"* Dr. Dzugan explains with logical arguments why health care is not free and what should be done to make it free again. His statement *"The problem with the current conventional medical model is that it does not focus on the actual root cause of many diseases and health conditions, but instead goes after the symptoms."* is 100% true. Hence, new approaches should be considered. Dr. Dzugan does outline this new philosophy in his book.

In Part III – *"On the Nature and Effects of Hormones,"* we are learning of the importance of hormones and their precursors such as DHEA, pregnenolone and testosterone. Dr. Dzugan clarifies the fact why bioidentical hormones are the best physiological option with hormone deficiencies and why synthetic hormones such as particular estrogens can increase the risk for cancer development. High testosterone levels are associated with decreased prostate cancer risk, and high levels prior to the occurrence of prostate cancer resulted in improved survival rates. This is really good news for many people.

In Part IV – *"On the Nature of the Restorative Approach,"* the reader learns about Dr. Dzugan's concept of his diagnostic and therapeutic approach. I fully agree with his philosophy *"that any human being is an individual and should be treated individually."* He does not put all people in one pot and does not treat them all with the same blood pressure medications and statins.

In Part V "On the Nature of Cholesterol," he demonstrates convincingly with a number of solid examples that lowering Cholesterol does more harm than cure. High cholesterol does not cause atherosclerosis, and any reputable source will make sure to specify this distinction. Lowering high cholesterol blood levels will make cells more fragile, damage muscle cells and the heart and reduces the production of our sex hormones. Hence lowering cholesterol may lead to erectile dysfunction and reduced libido.

In Part VI "On the Nature of Issues and Disease Related to Physiologic Breakdown," Dr. Dzugan explains why and how certain health issues can be solved by following a physiological approach. If substitution of a certain hormone is necessary then it should be the right and biological one. He explains what treatment he suggests for coronary heart disease, macular degeneration, fibromyalgia and migraine and why.

In Part VII "On the Nature of Nutrition and Health," he presents his view on how we can get fit and healthy again by life style, diet and exercise. *"A healthy digestive system is key to a healthy body,"* is his key message. He asks the question: *"Is fast food by nature and widespread practice unhealthy?"* His answer is: *"Yes, it is."* I have nothing to add in this regard.

This book, written in an entertaining and witty style, is a must for health conscious people, which most Americans are. Yet physicians can also learn a lot of Dr. Dzugan's physiological approach in solving health problems. This book could become an essential guide for anyone who wants to stay healthy and live long.

****

Professor George Birkmayer MD PhD
Ph.D. in Biochemistry, University of Vienna, Austria
M.D. from the University of Munich
Since 1982 Professor for Medical Chemistry, University of Graz, Austria.
Medical Director of the Birkmayer Institute for Parkinson Therapy, Vienna, Austria.
Visiting Professor at the Universities of Beijing, Guangzhou and Xi'An (China)
Fellow of the American College of Nutrition,
President Intl. Academy of Tumour Marker Oncology (IATMO) New York.
Professor George Birkmayer, M.D., Ph.D, discovered the therapeutic effect of NADH (Coenzyme-1) and developed the stabilized orally absorbable form of NADH. Using this formulation he has treated thousands of patients suffering from Parkinson, Alzheimer, depression, CFS, cancer and diabetes. He is the author of more than 150 scientific publications, and member of the editorial board of a number of scientific journals

INTRODUCTION

Medicine is a complex beast, of that we are all sure. Looking at all the intricacies of the vast modern medical complex can make your head spin. It is a great asset for the health of millions, billions even, across the world. It is the way in which we approach the treatment of disease and help people get better.

But there are certain chinks in the seemingly impregnable armor of conventional medicine. In certain cases it has fallen far because it focuses not on preventing the disease or disorder before it breaks out but instead on trying to control the symptoms after the fact. Such an approach might not seem like the best, you might say.

So what does that have to do with this physiological approach? Physiology is in reference to how the body functions under optimal circumstances. A variety of factors can lead to the slow decrease in adequate body function which can lead to a great deal of issues and diseases. What are the applications of this?

Too many to count. Imagine your body working fine. Now imagine it not working fine. Yeah, it isn't a very pretty picture. As we age more and more unfortunate issues start to crop up ranging from heart disease and high cholesterol to declining mental function. We become more fatigued, our body doesn't want to work likes supposed to, things which are supposed to stay up would rather stay down, and the list goes on. How does the restoration of human physiology work?

Well, by restoring the human physiology of course! This natural approach takes into account a multitude of subsystems that need to be fixed so that the body is rejuvenated to what we enjoyed in our 20s, instead of dreading how we feel each day in our 60s or 70s. This restoration of that which makes a fully functioning human work like a well-oiled machine is approached purely from a natural direction with no pharmaceutical intervention. What can be gained from this?

A lot. Recall all the "age related" diseases that afflict so many people just because people say that they are getting "old." This doesn't have to be the case. Age related diseases and impairments are in large part related to the gradual decline in our physiology. By going to town on the cause of the breakdown, rather than trying to fix what keeps being impaired by the breakdown, improvements can be achieved that not only greatly improve health but also benefit quality of life.

In this narrative we will be looking at a lot of different things, all framed with the restoration of physiological function in mind. We will observe how medicine shaped up and what are some of the problems we can associate with the conventional approach. We can see where conventional medicine overwhelmingly succeeds across a large sector of healthcare and places where it could use a hand. We will discuss at length the science behind physiologic decline and how it can be restored. We will also look at some of the diseases and issues associated with this breakdown such as heart disease, high cholesterol, psychological disease, and many other issues which can be approached in this natural way. Above all we want to present as much information as we can in the best way possible so that you yourself can have a better understanding of how our bodies work.

THE RESTORATION OF THE HUMAN BODY
IN SEVEN PARTS

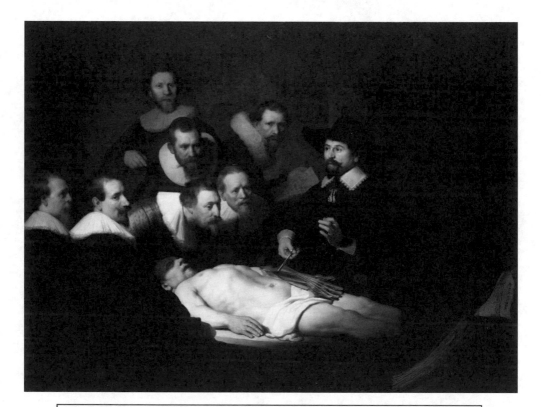

A Doctor teaches his students by dissecting a corpse. While our standards of science have advanced greatly, our neck frills and hats have unfortunately not followed suit.

PART I

On the History of Medicine and the Nature of Disease

What is medicine? Well, the answer to that one is probably quite obvious, isn't it? Medicine is the proverbial art of healing, that oldest of traditions where individuals, usually doctors, who know more than you tell you what to do so you can (probably) get better. But then there are so many different phrases thrown around in the air concerning medicine that it can become a bit of a pain to juggle them all and make sense out of all the bedlam.

For example, there is our dear old brother "conventional medicine," that beautiful majestic beast who holds fast with science, studies, and successes. He is held up as a trusted beacon of "making people feel better" and being an ever advancing juggernaut by virtue of acting as a cure for innumerable disease and ailments. Globalization doesn't hurt either. So, conventional medicine is big boss in the world of the healing arts, and all those "alternative," shady guys can't be trusted right?

And here the door opens and our friend the status quo (the concept, not the well-known band hailing from the United Kingdom) enters and he says, nay he yells - "Get these hippies off the doorstep of our majestic palace of conventional medicine, built from years of experience and learning. We need not your powdered keratin from certain odd toed ungulates or your exotic herbs of horny goats to cure our erectile dysfunction, for we are blessed by the powers that be with the glorious $C_{22}H_{30}N_6O_4S$. As you plebes might know of it, the blue pill!"

And with this mighty proclamation, the status quo stands firm, conventional medicine is superior, and all is well in the world. The unwashed masses of "the rest of those guys" are swept away by the power and logic of conventional medicine. After all, the opposite of conventional is unconventional! While the mighty well-oiled conventional army is fighting the good fight, the unconventional forces are rabble rousing guerrilla fighters in the bush, and who wants those guys on our side?

Terminology, the status quo, the court of public opinion, patents, and everything else surrounding conventional medicine seems to reinforce the fact that being big boss isn't simply given, it is taken by that which works and is the most powerful, which would also label it the most useful. Perhaps we can rewind time and see what is conventional and "unconventional" throughout the ages. Maybe by starting from the start, we can figure out where medicine stands.

Caveman Cures

We can begin not in olden days, but with a detour to our animal friends. What's this, you might ask, why in the world are we talking about animals? Well, the thing is that medicine as a concept is not the sole domain of humankind. Various monkeys have herbal remedies for relieving menstrual cramps, elephant mothers eat the bark of certain trees to induce labor, and pet house cats sneak out to eat grass when they are not plotting our downfall. These examples are certainly not all of them, and on top of the ones observed by humans, there are certainly other animal "medical" practices out there. But enough about those guys, we are going to talk about humans.

If we are speaking medicine, our collective memories as human beings might probably almost immediately go back to those Greek pioneers of this very field. Because clearly, every child in Samoa has a rich cultural history passed down in oral tradition of those crafty Greeks (thanks, globalization). The reason we think of the Greeks is because conventional medicine is also "western medicine," and as such we probably look to our toga wearing brothers and sisters as the progenitors of medicine.

But, as we just said, animals are taking all kinds of great herbs for all kinds of things. What does that have to do with anything? One would presume that most humans (on average) are smarter than most animals. Just don't say that anywhere a raven can hear you (which is everywhere). What this means is that ever since humans took the distinction of being the smartest mammals on the block, we didn't just magically form our own taxonomic classification with fresh new things and an exquisite knowledge of medicine, but rather built it up.

Knowledge about those good herbs was certainly passed down and utilized, especially with oral traditions and learning. As soon as *Homo neanderthalensis* Bobby took note that a certain plant cured his diarrhea, he would certainly pass this key information along to his mammoth hunting brethren. He either did that or kept the information to seize power and become chief, and we aren't here to judge Bobby's power hungry ambitions.

In archaeological excavations of "early" man during periods when ceremonial burial is documented, certain things are noted among the dead. In one particular dig site dubbed Shanidar Cave in northern Iraq, remains were found that conveyed significant information about their owners. One set of remains showed an individual missing a lower arm, with one potential cause being amputation, as well as a pretty severe crushing blow to the skull.

Looks like Neanderthal Bobby had an accident and perished then? Actually, based on the remains, both of these unfortunate events occurred well before death, and our Neanderthal friend potentially reached his late 40s. While late 40s is an early sendoff in our time, back in the olden days when ol' daddy had to fend off saber teethed tigers and Austrian barbarians, this would be considered grandfather age, telling his Neanderthal grandchildren about how good he had it before he lost that part of his arm and had that crushing injury happen to his face no doubt from those jerk *Homo sapiens* who just moved in to the cave just over that hill there.

Another set of remains found in this site shows an individual with advanced osteoarthritis, meaning they didn't just put him out to pasture when they noticed he wasn't keeping up with the mammoth hunting party. Such indicators show a significant level of care applied to individuals after either traumatic injury or debilitating conditions. There is also the significant fact that this site is dated between 60,000 to 80,000 BC (radio-carbon dating is a fickle mistress, but what's 20,000 years between old friends). For those keeping track at home, this is at least about 59,000 years before the Greeks were doing all their fancy Greek things for which we remember them for, and we don't mean the Spartan toga parties. Don't forget, these aren't *Homo sapiens* but rather *Homo neanderthalensis,* who are our "caveman" cousins.

The most important thing to take away from this is that this site is one that we have actually found. This is certainly not an isolated incident of altruistic individuals taking care of their sick. We can only have so many individuals who saw movies about courageous hat wearing archeologists go out to dig for ancient remains and societies, so a lot of things we don't know about. How far back medicine truly goes is a mystery to be sure, because while medicine might have been slowly accumulated as a knowledge databank, empathy towards other humans has been around for a whole lot, in most cases anyway. Certainly empathy would have made Bobby share the diarrhea cure with his friends (or not, but again, we aren't going to judge because maybe someone said something bad about his mammoth hide yurt that he put a lot of work into).

Erudite Egyptians and Persian Physicians

Now that we've covered the fact that medicine has roots deep in prehistory and even almost certainly before mankind itself, we can move on to those Greeks. But, those philosophers and democracy spreaders are going to have to get in line again, because Egypt had become a unified kingdom by 3150 BC, a decent bit before well-muscled Spartans (and a couple thousand of those "other" Greeks forgotten by popular lore) held the line at the Battle of Thermopylae. However, Egypt was a long standing kingdom with many individuals, so for our medicinal historic purposes, we can focus on one individual: Imhotep.

When many today think of Imhotep, they think of a mighty Egyptian who had an affair with the Pharaoh's concubine, raised the dead and caused plagues, and fought handsome actors in order to control the world. While Hollywood might have embellished on several "key aspects," it cannot be denied that Imhotep was an extremely intelligent and influential man. On top of building the first true stepped pyramid with uncanny mathematical accuracy (contrary to popular belief, there is more to building a pyramid than "putting a bunch of stones on top of each other,") he was also somewhat of a medicinal wizard as well.

Writings attributed to Imhotep's knowledge of medicinal expertise point to a detailed knowledge of disease and cures. While our knee jerk reaction might be to think that the best kept secret in ancient Egyptian "medicine" would be to pray to Anubis to not take the patient too soon, records indicate that Imhotep had what we can call case studies for prospective students about how to properly heal grievous head injuries that penetrate the

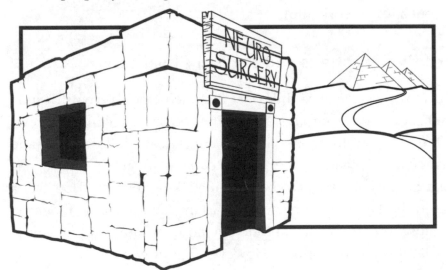

brain, among many other procedures. That's right; when Imhotep wasn't building pyramids and raising the dead, apparently he had a knack for brain surgery as well, at around 2600 BC. Based on such evidence it might even be prudent to say that Imhotep could even supplant Hippocrates as a well-known "father of medicine," but westernization has status quo to shout at anyone who would disagree. Also, Hippocrates has the distinction of being the "father of Western medicine," because clearly Imhotep is a bit "south" of "west".

Hippocrates the Greek, then, is well known today because doctors still swear the Hippocratic Oath when they become fully fledged in their profession. Though the full original is not particularly used now, the overall ideal of "do no harm" is a concept that is always very strong in this oath. While the medical understandings of Hippocrates weren't exactly what we would call up to par with our modern knowledge (but of course hindsight is always 20/20), he did establish that disease has natural origins and as such treatments or at the very least a study can be made of them, which was a very important idea because it allowed us to treat disease better knowing that Poseidon won't drown us with a flood for tampering with his curses. For this reason the concept of "modern" medicine really took off at this point.

A major idea behind medicine from this period and onward was the concept of "humors," which stated that there were 4 major humors. These humors were blood, black bile, yellow bile, and phlegm. They were also linked to the seasons and to the "4 elements" of air, earth, wind and fire. You can probably see where this is going. "Hah, what outdated and silly notions," you might think. Unfortunately, said silly notions persisted until the 1800s. So, medical knowledge based around the balancing of humors associated with the concept of 4 elements persisted for the majority of "conventional" medicine, and there is not much humorous about that. If the local physician told us that our touch of the tuberculosis was due to an unbalanced composition between air and water, you might say we would be concerned.

Medical history in general seems to be accomplished in bursts by particularly talented individuals. We can move right on through Medieval medicine by saying that, boy, are you lucky you weren't sick back then, at least in mainland Europe. If you were in the "Middle East" and Imhotep's old abode, your chances were actually better. A lot of good medical knowledge in the Medieval period actually arose not from Europe but Arabic doctors such as Ibn al-Nafis (full name being of course Ala-al-din abu Al-Hassan Ali ibn Abi-Hazm al-Qarshi al-Dimashqi, as we're sure everyone knows), who was the first known to describe pulmonary circulation (the novel concept of the heart pumping oxygen depleted blood to the lungs and returning back with oxygenated blood) in the mid-1200s, and Abu al-Qasim al-Zahrawi, who wrote an encyclopedic collection of medical practices and is sometimes referred to as the father of modern surgery, circa 1000 AD.

Belgian Breakthroughs and English Epidemiologists

Medicine didn't really get very much further until around the 1500s, when a Flemish doctor by the name of Andreas Vesalius published a comprehensive book on anatomy (called *De humani corporis fabrica libri septem*, otherwise known as *On the fabric of the human body in seven books*, because back then everything was in Latin and you had to make it count) that sought to improve on the many Greek errors by following actual illustrations of dissections and creating a valuable anatomical map of the human body. Though Andreas made mistakes in anatomical comprehension as well, we can cut the guy a break because in the 1500s we were still grappling around the concept of a heliocentric model of Earthly orbit. Slowly but surely, medicine had nowhere to go but up. Well, slowly up, but up somewhat nonetheless.

The 1700s saw such events as the first successful appendectomy (a minor procedure now) and the fact that citrus fruit cured scurvy (much to the relief of pirates and sailors who didn't need to have their gums bled anymore). During this century the procedure of vaccinations began to take root in Europe. While this is the well-known beginning of the history of vaccination for many, there were records of the procedure in India in the 800s (complete with a concept describing microbe action in theory), but westernization won't hear any of that. While microorganisms were "discovered," as in actually observed under the scrutiny of a microscope, by the late 1600s, the theory linking germs to disease didn't get properly established as a wide held "belief" until the later 1800s via the works of Robert Koch and Louis Pasteur. When introduced, this outlandish notion was "highly controversial" in the medical and scientific community.

As we round the end of the 1800s and go full blast into the 1900s, the pieces all start falling into place and are far too numerous to list, having already skipped over previous historical entries in the interest of time. After all, we simply wanted a brief overview of the history of medicine to see how conventional medicine evolved.

And did it ever! Thankfully now we don't need to be bled for every ailment or have our foot chopped off by a medieval doctor because that lesion on our toe looks borne of witchcraft. Now we have advanced surgical procedures and all the pills we could ever dream of! However, through that short jaunt through history, one thing has to be remembered. Conventional medicine hardly seems conventional in the long run.

For example, the dastardly notion that surgical instruments need to be disinfected and hands must be washed was an unconventional proposition by Joseph Lister which is now an integral part of modern surgical and medical procedure. The unconventional and alternative only becomes the conventional when enough individuals recognize that they are very viable treatments that work on a fundamental level. Unfortunately, while conventional, modern medicine is certainly a great benefit to humanity and part of the reason as to why we spit in the face of Malthusian population checks, there are certain areas of it that are not utilized to the best extent based around the core tenants of medicine.

To go fully in depth and further with this, we have to identify the major causes of disease and illness. Before proceeding, we need to clarify the catch all term of disease. For example, both AIDS and depression are disease. However, it would be more adequate to describe AIDS as an infectious disease while we can describe depression as a mental disorder. Only by understanding our enemy, can we fight the enemy, and so on and so forth. We can simplify all disease into infectious and non-infectious, and we can further divide the second into two subcategories, with a special guest star at the end that will lead into the main focus of our discussions regarding restorative medicine.

Of Vectors and Viruses

Infectious disease is the one that many of us think of when the word disease itself is mentioned. These are the diseases that are "catching" and are spread via vectors. A vector is an organism that transmits the disease, such as mosquitoes for malaria or us when we don't cover our mouth in a crowded elevator when we have a touch of the Spanish Flu, because hey it's totally not bad manners or a crime against hygiene and mankind to do that.

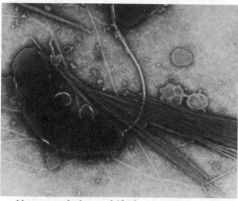

Hey guy, is it cool if I hang out here?

While it would be nice to think that there is an innumerable host of microscopic organisms out there that want us dead, this isn't really a fair assumption. Also, that isn't a very nice picture at all. What we can say is that it is all relative. Consider cholera. Vibrio cholerae just wants to breed uncontrollably and do the thing that all living organisms want, to live and prosper. Unfortunately, to live and prosper further, cholera has figured out that the side effect of violent diarrhea and vomiting is going to spread more cholera to more people. Cholera by no means wants us to die, it just wants to spread as far as it can. Technically speaking, the most successful infectious microorganism is the one that keeps the host alive as long as possible.

The only problem is those pesky side effects which are the manifestations of the disease which might tend to cause us to die, which neither of us want. But cholera goes and ruins it for everyone, wanting too much of a good thing. Planet Earth is probably saying right now "Yeah, Mars, I've had this case of the humans for a long time but the little buggers have really been a pain in the last couple of centuries. This is worse than the time Theia collided with me and formed that jerk the Moon."

Relativity aside, what we want to do is kill the invaders because we are humans and that's how we take care of business. In the cholera example, we can look at bacteria, with bacteria being one of the four antagonists when we are speaking about infectious disease. Disease caused by bacteria includes cholera, typhus, bacterial meningitis, bacterial pneumonia, and the list goes on. Bacteria can be killed off by the appropriately named antibiotics. However, the extremely fast division and growth of bacteria allows for relatively fast evolutionary processes which in turn allow them to eventually adapt to antibiotics. Antibiotic resistant bacteria pose a serious issue because more powerful antibiotics have to be used until in some cases they simply stop working. Good news for them, bad news for us. As far as harmful bacteria are concerned, over the counter antibiotics are the best things to ever happen for them.

Fungal infections are those caused by fungi. While we may laugh about athletes foot in the locker room, fungal infections can become a pretty serious matter. Some fungi can cause forms of pneumonia and meningitis, which are a bit rougher than a bad case of athlete's foot. Black mold, other than having a name appropriate for something that lives in a city built of nightmares, grows in damp places and can cause serious respiratory infections. The problem with this one is that said damp places usually happen to be homes, with people breathing in the mycotoxins (toxins produced via the metabolism of molds). The route of attack against fungi are appropriately named antifungal drugs (we're beginning to see a pattern here). Much like bacteria, fungi can become resistant to these drugs, but instead of a good basket of truffles, it results in a heaping portion of disease that is resistant to drug therapy.

Parasitic infections need to be clarified first. A parasitic relationship is one where the parasite lives in or with the host in a non-mutual fashion, just like that son who is totally going to eventually go back to college to get a degree in communications and will certainly move out when he is done (and he totally won't stay home to play online games and eat all your food after that). Not only do they not pay the rent, but they slowly set the house on fire. Thus, the previously listed examples can already be classified as parasitic. In the context of infectious diseases, parasitic infections are those referring to human parasites such as protozoa and worms. Suffice to say, the disease caused by many parasites are pretty disgusting so we can avoid talking about those, because worms need to stay in the ground and away from our bodies. However, we can mention malaria, which needs no introduction and causes more than half a million deaths per year in the tropics. While mosquitoes are a vector, the actual cause is the protist transferred via saliva during a bite. The treatment of parasites is as varied as the parasites themselves.

The last well known villain at the theater is the virus. If we were still speaking in Medieval European terms, we could call the virus an unholy manifestation of all that is wrong. The virus is one that has us confused because it isn't exactly something that we can with certainty call a living thing. While it replicates and evolves, it lacks

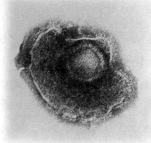

I'll just be over here, ancient and eternal.

cellular structure and reproduces by spontaneous assembly with the host cells without even having the decency to asexually split. It would seem that as life came into being, the virus didn't get the memo and simply said "Nah you guys go ahead, I'm gonna go over here and do my own thing." One would imagine this would have barred the virus from all the good parties, which is why it now has a tendency to cause some of the most serious and resilient diseases known to man.

Examples of viruses range far and wide. While cold sores are considered little more than a nuisance, the variant of herpes that causes it is quite widespread, and transmission can even occur when the cold sore is not present. It is not very comforting that this variant of herpes infects more people in the world than it doesn't, and is just content to stay in our bodies until death. AIDS needs no introduction and is caused by HIV. Our yearly friend influenza, better known as the flu, is also caused by a virus. Certain chronic viruses can also cause cancer in infected victims, because clearly viruses aren't horrifying enough. Primary antiviral treatments include antiviral drugs, as antibiotics do not work as per the popular misconception, and vaccinations are an effective method of preventing viruses as well.

That finishes the brief rundown of infectious diseases. One important thing to keep in mind is that the manifestation of infectious diseases is the way in which the microscopic invaders interact with our body. For example, our old friend pneumonia is the disease associated with inflammation of the lungs followed hand in hand with coughing, sharp pain in the chest - the works so to speak. This is the disease. The actual cause? Whatever you want.

Pneumonia can be caused by bacteria, fungi, parasites, and those unholy manifestations of un-life the viruses. So, let's say you get vaccinated against a type of bacterial pneumonia (as in you are vaccinated against that particular microbe from causing this particular type of pneumonia) and you are itching for a fight with this disease. Well, you would be winning that particular fight and be impenetrable until a virus infiltrates your body and causes the disease anyway, because you are not inoculated against this viral pneumonia, or simply put the virus that causes that pneumonia.

Of Schizophrenia and Scurvy

True to its name, a non-infectious disease is one that does not spread through a vector. Even in the case of the aforementioned cancer by way of virus does not fall under this category, because the virus can cause cancer, but the cancer is not the infectious disease. So what about these non-infectious diseases then?

Well, they are quite the handful. Seeing the extent of infectious disease, we can then throw in all the rest of the players on the island into the category of non-infectious disease. But first, we must separate them into disease caused by genes and those caused by environmental factors. Genetics can be looked at first because from the standpoint of definitions we can more readily assess it.

Diseases caused by malfunctioning genes are more properly called genetic disorders. While Down syndrome is technically a disease, nobody calls it Down disease. Down syndrome is caused when there is extra genetic material on the 21st chromosome (a structure of DNA and proteins, of which we have 23 in total). Down syndrome is characterized by various defects as well as an increased likelihood for other conditions. Individuals with Down syndrome are at an increased risk of having congenital heart disease, as an example. Another example of a purely genetic disease is cystic fibrosis, an ailment where multiple organs, specifically the lungs, cannot function properly.

Genetic disease is not linked solely to congenital defects that are present from day one. Diseases with a genetic influence work out in that the genes are passed down from your forebears. In other words, them having said disease is an expression of genetic likelihood of that gene "running in the family." There is a wide assortment of diseases that you can acquire through increased genetic probability passed down. For example, if your father had voices in his head telling him to kill Adolf Hitler, we can surmise two things: that the voices were on the right track, and that you might wind up with schizophrenia.

The previous mention of congenital heart disease in Down syndrome patients is something that is very important to mention when we're speaking about non-infectious disease with our two separations of genetic and environmental. Congenital heart disease can arise purely from a genetic abnormality, ranging from DNA mutations to chromosomal irregularities. However, congenital heart disease can also occur from environmental factors, such as if the mother of the fetus partakes in alcohol during pregnancy or if she is afflicted with certain diseases. Even the aforementioned schizophrenia can result from environmental factors.

With this we can go further in depth with environmental disease, because at the end of the day there is little we can further say on purely genetic diseases other than "Man, some stuff is going to get messed up outside of your control and then this will happen." The medical field of gene therapy is still in its relative infancy and far from having mass market consumption, but with increased testing and technology is certainly promising.

Environmental disease is the impossibly broad definition of diseases caused by the environment. We aren't saying that the plants in your local biosphere are out to get you (but some of them just might be,) but instead are classifying the "environmental" factors as anything living or nonliving that has an impact on living organisms (which is redundant, because all organisms are by definition living, and viruses can stay well away with their vile sorcery).

Let's take a deeper look at non-genetically influenced schizophrenia as a good example of the variety present in environmental factors, having covered increased genetic probability already. There are some studies that bear mention in our example here because they clearly reinforce our earlier environmental distinction. "The environment" does not mean the type of trees and the fauna that exist in your neck of the woods, or whether you live in a temperate broadleaf forest biome or a wet riparian biome. At least, not specifically. The environment is the sum of the parts of the location where you live.

Let's say that you are residing in New York City. That means that you currently live in a temperate broadleaf forest. But last time we checked, "skyscraper" is not a part of the natural temperate broadleaf forest biome. So, we can easily say that you live in the "urban" environment. And if you grow up in said urban environment, your risk of acquiring schizophrenia increases a decent amount simply by virtue of growing up in this urban area.[1] To add salt to the wound, it appears that if you are a member of an immigrant ethnic group and not a native born individual, living in areas of low same ethnicity concentration, you are at higher risk of schizophrenia down the line.[2-4]

While the link is tenuous, there is the possibility that the use of cannabis is associated with increased risks for psychotic disorders and symptoms.[5] However, one link that is certainly not tenuous is the predisposition of individuals with pre-existing risk of psychosis to the states induced by cannabis use than that of healthy control subjects.[6,7] While these are actual assessment or control studies, there is certainly no end of anecdotal evidence that while some individuals who partake of the marijuana fly up high on the back of magical dragons and become unstoppable hunger machines, others succumb to paranoia.

In one fell swoop we examined several examples of environmental factors, but perhaps we put too much emphasis on the actual environment that a person lives in. In the interest of diversity, we can take a good look at some other examples of environmental factors. Earlier on during our brief run through the history of medicine, we briefly mentioned scurvy. While it may be known simply as the bane of pirates, for most of human history scurvy has actually been a pretty serious concern for all ocean expeditions and long winters full of cured meats. What is the environmental factor at work here?

The long voyages or time periods with a lack of fresh produce necessitated the storage of food that was cured, salted, or in the form of hardtack rations that could probably be used as bricks if the sailors weren't up to eating tooth breaking month old biscuits. After the link between citrus fruits was established, would this have been the environmental factor that causes scurvy? Lack of oranges and lemons? We now know that vitamin C deficiency is at play here, and those fruits simply happened to have a ready supply of it.

But again, we cannot stress enough that environmental factors are part of the "anything goes" category, and not just related to deficiencies of something or variables outside of our control. Rampant tobacco smoking can lead to chronic obstructive pulmonary disease, which is the ever potent combination of chronic bronchitis and emphysema. The environmental risk at work here is inhalation of tobacco smoke, which is wholly dependent (outside of uncontrollable second hand exposure) on the individual in question. But even then, certain individuals are still more susceptible to acquire this disease due to the genetic factor. [8]

Type 2 diabetes has strong environmental components in both obesity and lack of physical activity. Surely, you might think, that if you simply keep those two at bay, type 2 diabetes will steer clear of you. But consider an individual who has a genetic defect that hinders physical activity, or who has a genetic predisposition towards obesity. Let's spice up the mix even more and say that both of those can also be caused in part or in whole by an infectious disease. This is all on top of the known genetic factors at work in acquiring type II diabetes (of which about 10% are known, meaning that 90% of the genetic issues that can influence risk factors are unknown).[9]

What is evident at the end of the day is that there is a lot of interplay between the types of disease, and many issues can bounce off of each other to create an ultimately more serious condition. In the midst of all these environmental disease is where the bulk of our focus comes in. What we want to look at and discuss is disease that is caused by **acquired physiologic errors**. Physiologic simply refers to a normally functioning and healthy body, with physiology itself being the science of this.

What are diseases caused by acquired physiologic errors? This is going to come out of left field and include a good bunch, so bear with us. Issues such as heart disease, depression, arthritis, fibromyalgia, migraine, fatigue, atherosclerosis, and cancer can all fall under this category.

An approach of restorative medicine, which is what we will be discussing from this point on, focuses on addressing the break downs of optimal body function by optimizing the body's hormones and nutrients to optimal levels. While the body at all times tries to keep in homeostasis (equilibrium), things are going to break and it will happen. When the balance and ratios of hormones within the body breaks down, along with a lack of minerals and vitamins, then things will go south real fast.

"Oh boy here we go," you might think. "This old boy is talking about curing cancer by keeping my body's 'hormones' in check and making sure I eat my oranges. I'm beginning to suspect he's actually one of those alternative guys he made fun of in the beginning. No doubt next I'll be advised to buy some crystals that are attuned to my body's electromagnetic output."

This is where our old friend simplification hurls a rabbit punch to our neck and distinctions need to be made. The statement that "this thing in balance will keep this thing from happening" doesn't take into account the staggering complexity of what goes on in our bodies. Also, at this juncture we would certainly specify that having a fully optimized physiological profile is a part of avoiding certain cancers and in general as part of an adequate immune response, which is influenced in large part by the hormones that we will be discussing in detail later. However, if Uncle Boris goes playing around the nuclear reactor, then he is going to get cancer no matter how good his testosterone level is because lethal doses of radiation and cellular matter don't like to mingle. Contrary to popular belief, Vodka does not cure radiation poisoning. So let's amend that cancer listing as "cancers that your body is fully capable of keeping at bay with an optimized physiologic profile if everything is in balance and working A-OK."

One Malaise, One Route of Attack

This restorative approach to medicine is an effective method of treating disease and ailments acquired by physiologic errors because ultimately they are basically the same disease. This obviously seems like a foreign concept from the get go because conventional medicine creates very clear separations between diseases. How can we imply that something like heart disease is the same as migraine, osteoporosis, or depression? What we are suggesting is that at a basic level they are the same because they have the same issue of suboptimal and unbalanced hormones, as well as vitamins and minerals.

One might scoff at the notion of vitamins and minerals, and perhaps rightfully so, that is if all we followed in our health related world view was popular notions and misconceptions. Let's not forget our friend scurvy, the vitamin C deficiency. If you are enjoying not having your gums bled in pirate tradition, you can thank the adequate vitamin C in your diet. Adequate iron in your diet helps stave off a common form of anemia (a condition where your blood does not have enough red blood cells, which most scholars agree is a good thing to have).

Adequate iodine intake helps the thyroid gland function properly, and one of the jobs of the thyroid gland is to manage how sensitive the body is to its own hormones. Lack of iodine in a mother's diet can cause the birth of children who grow up to be mentally and physically retarded without intervention (no intervention being the usual case, because if the mother cannot procure adequate iodine in her diet in her environment, the child will likely experience it

as well), and lack of iodine during infant development can cause mental retardation as well. Overall, iodine deficiency is by far the most preventable cause of brain damage and mental retardation in the entire world.[10] Next time you're at the local grocery store, make sure to stop by the iodized salt and say thanks, because he's been looking out for you.

We could certainly go further in detail on this matter, but for now we just wanted a cursory glance to dispel preconceived notions. "Make sure you get your vitamins and minerals" as a phrase has become almost hackneyed and somewhat jokey, something parents might say to their kids perhaps without even enforcing it themselves. We make an effort to eat "healthy" foods but usually forget the reason healthy food is classified as such. It is not only because it has low fat content or lacks excessive amounts of sugar, but also because of the beneficial vitamins and minerals that it contains.

But surely, you might ask, even with a basic root cause, wouldn't certain disease be caused by imbalances of different areas and necessitate a specific treatment approach? Wouldn't heart disease be caused by a certain imbalance while something such as depression be caused by another one? Yes and no.

What we mean by one treatment approach has to be looked at not at face value and in the conventional sense for it to not sound ridiculous. This is because of what we associate with the word treatment based on conventional medicine. What sort of treatment do I get if I have high cholesterol? You take this pill. What sort of treatment do I get when I have depression? You take this other pill. What treatment do I get if I have type 2 diabetes? You take this insulin, you watch your blood sugar, you make sure to exercise, and in general you avoid behavior that can exacerbate your condition. Now we are getting somewhere.

A lot of conventional treatment operates on a 1:1 basis, where you have one thing and you take one thing from the pharmacy for it. Meanwhile, optimal human physiologic function has an extremely intricate network of links and dependencies that forces anyone who is trying to optimize it to not look at symptoms here and there but instead at the picture as a whole. When we are speaking of a restorative medicinal approach to the restoration of physiologic function, we throw the 1:1 approach out the window.

Instead, all the factors have to be considered. This is low and unbalanced. What do we have to do to increase that level, what else will this increase impact, how will this increase benefit another problem in the body, how will the other thing that we are already trying to improve affect the efficiency of this increase, and so on and so forth. Ultimately, it is most certainly a "one" treatment approach. It just so happens that said treatment seeks to cover every nook and cranny within the body's complex physiologic function.

So what about all this hormone stuff we're talking about? We will get to that and why they are so important, with guest appearance by big daddy cholesterol, and will look at all these diseases and conditions that arise from the breakdown of physiological function. We will certainly also look at the unfortunate reason these imbalances happen, where we can introduce our own approach to correcting these issues. The ultimate goal here is first and foremost the dissemination of information so that you can better understand how your own body works and how complex interaction can be understood and utilized to improve your function. But first... we discuss the pitfalls of conventional medicine. *Dramatic Fanfare*

Much like Saint George slaying the dragon, conventional medicine has taken out a lot of baddies. Unfortunately, a village or two might have been burned along the way.

PART II

On the Pitfalls of Conventional Medicine

No its okay, you can put the tinfoil hats and divining rods away, we haven't gone off the deep end. When we go and say something like "On the Pitfalls of Conventional Medicine," we are going to make well sure that the distinction is made on what we are talking about. We aren't going to use a blanket statement and say "Man that there conventional medicine is all goofed up," but instead we are going to focus on which parts of conventional medicine under which conditions have the mentioned pitfalls.

Conventional medicine as a whole is an amazing machine. We have eradicated the likes of polio and smallpox. We have turned diabetes from an extremely premature death sentence into a manageable disease. Millions of infants live today where just more than a century ago they would have been dead before their first day. We're even starting to give HIV a run for its money.

Now, if you go on a whimsical safari to sub-Saharan Africa to see some lions and giraffes and just happen to acquire Ebola, then several things are going to happen. First of all, no matter how good your hormones and body physiology is, Ebola doesn't play around. Now certainly, if your body physiology is optimized and your internal systems are rearing up and good to go, you could well be the potential 10% of people who don't die due to untreated Ebola.[1] But with 9:1 odds, our money is going to be on Ebola.

Second, you will get whisked away to a quarantined Ebola ward set up with emergency protocols in mind, where you might survive 32% of the time. While that might not sound like a reassuring number, we can thank conventional modern medicine for establishing the protocols, medication, and necessary research to fight whatever the microscopic world throws at us, as well as the necessary medicine to counteract the sometimes brutal damage such diseases can cause.

So, we've established that conventional medicine, at its core and through many points of its activity and healing methodology, is a very great thing. It generally keeps us living longer (we'll get right on that in a bit) and just makes things better all around. Now we're going to hit the lackluster part.

The problem with the current conventional medical model is that it does not focus on the actual root cause of many diseases and health conditions, but instead goes after the symptoms.

This is where we have to get technical and break it down. First of all, you must note the "many" and by no means "all." Let's say that a favored co-worker is trying to be "funny," and decides to send you an envelope filled with flour. You, being the culinary challenged individual, believe it not to be the potential gateway to unimaginable delicacies in the form of baked goods, but rather a heaping portion of anthrax spores. You run to the hospital to get checked out and are given a clean bill of health, while your co-worker is taken away to be water boarded in the defense of democracy. That'll teach him.

Suppose that you actually did contract anthrax, and *Bacillus anthracis* has gained a foothold in your body. What is going to happen if you rush for treatment? An extremely potent dose of antibiotics will be put in your body, both intravenously and orally. This treatment regimen will greatly increase your chance of survival depending on the type of, because this matchup, antibiotics versus the bacteria, is going after the root cause of the disease by "fixing" the issue that is causing it.

This is all good and demonstrates perfectly where the combination of the fruits of our scientific research in antibiotics and our works in epidemiology identifies the root cause of the disease and focuses on eliminating it to fix the problem. Hold on, you might think, but this is all related to infectious disease which is transferred by pathogenic action, while the diseases related to the breakdown of physiologic function that were mentioned earlier are all of the non-infectious environmental sort.

This is an excellent observation we didn't just put in your head because we wrote it (why the very notion)! Again, we have to shift our *specific* definition of disease. We already covered all those things that can cause coughs, involuntary body effluences, and oozing sores. From this point hence, whenever we refer to disease, we are referring to our particular subset, the familiar neck of the woods inhabited solely by disease caused by bodies that don't work properly due to the breakdown of physiologic function. This precise corner of the woods is from where we will launch our skirmishes against popular concepts and standards of the way that these diseases are currently "treated" in our medical system.

Heart Disease and Inadequate Mammoth Hunters

In 2011, the typical family of four in the United States spent $19,393 for healthcare (take that, communists). You might pensively nod your head in agreement, perhaps dropping a curse here and there about the "establishment." As with all numbers, relativity helps out for comprehension. After all, we can hear about the Milky Way galaxy being 100,000 light years across all day long, but until we realize that the distance from the Earth to the Sun is only 15.813×10^{-6} light years (it takes sunlight a little over 8 minutes to reach the Earth), it doesn't mean much. Back to our more worldly concerns of paying the doctor bills, we can look at 2009 and see that this same cost was $16,771. Meanwhile, those upstart youngsters in 2003 were enjoying a cost of $10,168.[2]

You might think as to what this has to do with our particular target diseases. After all, one does not simply walk into Congress and lower health care costs. This is true, and not the point of this data here. We listed these values because a staggering percentage of that money goes toward the treatment of preventable disease, specifically non-infectious disease (so we aren't bringing vaccines and anti-pathogens into this equation). In fact, coronary heart disease is the leading killer in the developed world.[3-5]

Let's talk about coronary heart disease. Studies are everywhere with this topic, but there are certain variables which remain constant. Specific post analysis of one particularly large study showed what variables mitigated risk and what variables increased risk. In this analysis, mild to moderate work related physical activity decreased the risk of myocardial infarction (death of heart cells due to interruption of blood supply), while owning a car and television increased the risks.[6]

Now, don't go throwing out the Toshiba and selling the Toyota just yet. Let's not forget our environmental catch all factors. Owning either of those items simply promotes sedentary behavior, and thus increasing the risk. You can probably see where this is going. If a person performs both regular physical activity and doesn't own a car or television, then he is less likely to be obese (because he is working very hard to afford a car and television).

That large study that this previous one focused in on is large indeed. It tracked 15,152 cases with 14,820 controls across 52 countries on every inhabited continent (Antarctica always gets left out, because everyone gives her the cold shoulder). The risk factors for myocardial infarctions in this study were established as abnormal lipids (which include fats and triglycerides), smoking, hypertension (high blood pressure), diabetes, obesity, psychosocial factors (we're looking at you, stress), consumption of fruits and vegetables, partaking of alcohol, and physical activity.[7]

As you can see, these factors are of the preventable variety. Putting out the smuggled Cuban cigar, hitting the gym, not being mistaken for the mall Santa or Mrs. Claus during Christmas time, and drinking less alcohol can give you much better odds. It seems that the developed countries have indeed developed more ways to not move around and how to add another flour and cornmeal layer to that fried chicken. The number one killer has never tasted so good. While we're on the subject of fried fowl, obesity is not only a high risk factor for coronary heart disease, but is also a big risk period. Much like heart disease, obesity is one of the leading causes of preventable death.[8] In fact, we can quickly deconstruct links to obesity and its role in myocardial infarction as per most of the risk factors that were mentioned.

❖ High blood pressure - there is a large association between obesity and elevated blood pressure.[9]

❖ Diabetes - obese individuals are at a high risk of acquiring type 2 diabetes.[10]

❖ Obesity - well we worked ourselves into a corner with this one.

❖ Psychosocial factors - this one is much more variable. In the not so distant past and in various cultures even today, obesity was and is associated with wealth, since only a wealthy individual could attain the excess calories in the form of abundant food or livestock needed to become and remain obese. In the present day in the "western" world, bacon sandwiches as far as the eye can see are available to the masses and obesity in general is seen primarily as a stigma. Being obese in a culture that is telling you not to be obese can cause extra stress for the individual.

❖ Consuming fruits and vegetables (eating healthy) - who in the world needs to eat healthy when we have double fried chicken and bacon sandwiches? Besides, pizza has olives on it (but we usually switch those out for extra Canadian bacon).

❖ Physical activity - while physical activity becomes more and more difficult the more obese one becomes, logic would dictate that perhaps it would be not a bad idea to not let it get that far in the first place. Word on the grapevine is that there is this fad going around called "ambulation," and supposedly all you have to do is get up and go somewhere. The world certainly is full of silly ideas.

❖ Alcohol Consumption - this link is more tenuous because it certainly isn't 1:1. However, one simply has to think back to the time when Big Jim and the boys are swigging back their 20th brew at the Cotton Fair to remember that basic alcohol consumption includes a lot of "empty" calories, promoting an entire industry of watered down beer and elastic waistband manufacturing. Being obese certainly doesn't make an individual drink, but the drinking itself can plant the seed for obesity in the first place as well as increasing its severity. It certainly doesn't help that this fermented ambrosia can be addictive.

The only others left on the list are smoking and lipids. Smoking is smoking and, despite the big warnings on the side of cigarette packets and the billboard extinction of beloved manly chain smoking cowboys, is still practiced by about 21% of Americans.[11] Supposedly lipids include that international felon cholesterol, but we're going to go into further detail about that later because it covers a very fair portion of coronary heart disease's main co-conspirator - atherosclerosis, which is also commonly paired with coronary heart disease. Atherosclerotic plaque thickens artery walls by building up on them, and a component of this plaque is cholesterol. That discussion will naturally include the role of restorative medicine regarding this condition and how it can benefit.

On the subject of obesity in the United States, more than one third (35.7%) of adults and 17% of children and adolescents are obese. If we consider a state by state analysis, data from 2010 shows that not a single state has less than a 20% obesity rate. If you traveled across the United States, at the very least about 21 out of every 100 people (Colorado) you meet will be obese, and in some states this number is as high as 34 out of every 100 people (Mississippi).[12] The "thinnest" state's population has an obesity rate higher than 1/5. We must also keep in mind that obese is obese. If an individual is under the standard classification of being just "slightly overweight," then they do not factor into those numbers. Our old friend Caveman Bobby would probably have some words to say about the dangers and futility of mammoth hunting while having a Body Mass Index (BMI) greater than 30. He might also point out that BMI is a very flawed sort of measurement, but that is neither here nor there.

With some knowledge behind our belt about this particular disease, let's consider how the mainstream conventional medical approach would work, it being a system of reactions in this case as opposed to a system focusing on prevention. Coronary artery bypass surgery is a technique of vein and artery grafting which improves blood circulation to heart muscle with a potential for the reduction of risk of death from coronary heart disease. However, while the benefit of performing this procedure on someone who is actually having a heart attack is known, the benefit for individuals with stable conditions is not established.

One particular study conducted over 5 years observed patients with coronary heart disease split into two major groups. One group was treated with medical therapy alone while the other was also treated with the bypass procedure. There was no observable difference in regards to total death in the two groups, although the group that had the procedure done had lower rates of death specifically from cardiovascular causes.[13]

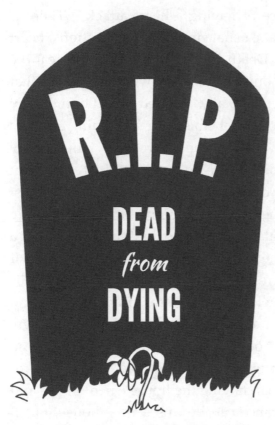

So, who won? While the second group did have less incidence of death from the cause that was targeted, the overall amount of death was indistinguishable. Dead is dead, as the saying goes. This is something we will be looking at in other instances as another potential pitfall of the conventional approach. Being targeted by a specific treatment for a condition and not dying from that condition for a population is good, but when the number of deaths within that population increases to as much from other causes or even to a higher rate while undergoing the treatment, the novelty of not dying from the first one quickly wears off.

Another player in the reactive conventional treatment game for coronary heart disease is angioplasty. This procedure involves threading a deflated balloon towards an atherosclerotic deposit and then inflating it, crushing the buildup to improve blood flow. A small tube called a stent may be placed in this location to ensure that it stays open. Both this procedure and the bypass can improve chest pain.[14] Unfortunately, it does not increase life span past what can be achieved with therapy nor does it decrease the chance of having a heart attack.[15] There is also the slight chance of your usual surgical complications, heart attack being one of them. Death isn't funny, but it sure can be ironic. At least we can tell our friends and loved ones about that one time when "that doctor totally inflated a balloon in my artery," which we hope isn't a euphemism for something else.

In 2006 alone, 1.3 million coronary angioplasty procedures were performed with an average cost of about $48,000 each and 448,000 coronary bypass surgeries at almost $100,000 each. Together, these two operations totaled a bit more than $100 billion in medical costs.[16] The main issue here is that a surgical intervention is a high cost, end of the line procedure. If even some of these funds from insurance companies, both public and private, were funneled more into preventative and restorative measures, then the overall cost would go down. Making sure that we turn off the stove before we go out and checking for electrical wiring faults are a whole lot cheaper (or free, as the case may be), than having the house catch on fire and burn to the ground. Insurance can buy us a new house, but it won't buy us a second life.

Fries versus Fiber

What about nutrition and healthy eating anyway? Since many of us go to the doctor to pilfer their minds of sound advice in all realms anatomical, one would expect that they have a wealth of advice to offer about good eating guidelines. Unfortunately, while medical school is quite a long ordeal, part of said long ordeal doesn't really involve learning about proper nutrition.

A 2007 study of 106 medical schools showed that only 30% of them required the students to take a separate nutrition course. The average amount of hours received of nutritional education (over the entirety of their school term) was 23.9, with the actual overall hours ranging from 2 to 70 (in other words, while some students got 70 hours of such an education, many got as little as 2 and brought that average down quite a bit).[17] Suffice to say, it doesn't appear that getting your fiber in and making sure to eat those leafy greens is priority one at the endurance ordeal that we call medical school.

But then, you might say, who cares? I hear doctor, I think of surgery and medication. The first is accurate, because while a doctor is not always a surgeon, a surgeon is always a doctor (or at least one would hope). The second is perhaps an unfortunate association. It is of course true, though, that a huge part of a doctor's training goes into learning how to cut someone open not in an effort to butcher but in an effort to save, as well as the pathways of disease and what medication can be used to help. After all, medication is the blanket term for anything that is used to help sick people get better, which would include vitally important items such as antibiotics and anti-viral drugs.

However, let's back up and look at the disease that can be caused by improper diet. Obesity and not eating well leads into hypertension, type 2 diabetes, coronary heart disease, and more. Let's not forget that some of those are leading killers and some would say that preventing death from disease is high up on the list of things to do for the medical profession. Thus, while we depend on the doctors to help improve our health, we have a high probability of a doctor who has little to none true education about nutrition despite their vast knowledge about their field.

So who can we turn to for nutritional advice? Grandma keeps telling us to eat our beets to not wind up like Grandpa during the Great War but we're not all that sure that's enough. Some health magazines and books have recipes but overall eating guidelines might be scant, not to mention the fact that the source must always be in question because a journalist isn't exactly high up on the list of people we wish to turn to for health advice. Let's not forget fad diets, because what can go wrong from 48 hours of juice drinking and fasting?

There are of course individuals who may even call their own profession "nutritionist," but that can be a touch sketchy. Many countries have no regulation (or regulation that varies by state or province) whatsoever on who can call themselves a nutritionist, and lack a system of pre-requisites or standardized practices. While one nutritionist may have a vast background of encyclopedic knowledge and sound advice about many food types backed up by training from an accredited source, another nutritionist might tell you to eat barley for a week straight because "It's totally good for you, man." In this case the lowest common denominator brings everybody down and many

individuals might be liable to see nutritionists just a step above "hedge wizard" in the helpful profession category. Although, if that hedge wizard can make potions for weight loss, then clearly he would be the better choice.

While the nutritional advice and hedge wizard field is highly likely to improve as preventable disease keep killing, to some it might not be the best consolation. After all, we go to the doctor to cut us open and graft extra tissue to our hearts to not extend our life expectancy, so we would expect that same doctor to be able to explain to us about eating right 10 years prior to help avoid that operation in the first place. Both of these things apply to disease, and "D" is for disease, but also for doctor.

Jerky Knees and Potent Prescriptions

Ah, meds. As a consumer society, we love us some drugs, as they say in the vernacular. Why, there are pills for everything you could ever dream of! There are diet pills that most certainly don't make us feel like transdimensional warriors separated from our body to feel no hunger or emotion, and we certainly are not describing that from any personal experience. If we feel blue, in a blue house, and everyone around is blue, there are certainly pills to add some additional colors to our world so that we can go out and perhaps go to Paris to see the Eiffel Tower like that time in 1965. There are even pills that help us apprehend that international fugitive, cholesterol. If we want to go out on the town and party, and by party we mean ordering the seven layered nachos filled with strata upon strata of melted cheese and potent peppers, then we have the meds to help us weather the initial digestive onslaught and the inevitable cataclysm of purging fire that follows the next morning as sure as the sun rises in the east.

The problem with such drugs, be they prescription or over the counter, is that they are not treating the base cause, the disease, but are instead trying to treat the symptoms. Let's say a dam has a crack in it and is slowly flooding the valley. Engineers come up with the brilliant plan of putting in great big pumps into the valley to suck all the water up while releasing heavy smoke into the air from the process, and everyone applauds this move as a wise decision. You might say that this sounds like it makes no sense and is perhaps even borderline illogical. What is the logical thing here? We get those engineers, we give them some steel and cement, and we get those boys to fix the dam.

While this may seem like quite the nonsensical example, it can be applied directly too many popular drug treatments today. We take a look at the underlying causes of disease, then say hah screw that, and then we go and start treating the symptoms. How is treatment accomplished? The simplest way possible - a trip to the pharmacy and a pill bottle. While taking the pill to treat the symptom, a symptom that isn't getting any better because the cause of the symptom is not being addressed, we are even likely to have side effects.

Instead of fixing our dams, we pollute the air and pump out the water, until that original crack grows big enough and the entire thing breaks and floods the valley even more. This is of course considering we don't choke on the smoke first. To see the prevalence of prescription drugs, one only needs to turn on the television and wait for a commercial break. The game is won as soon as an advertisement concerning prescription drugs comes on. We would not advise anyone to use this as the basis of a drinking game, however, because by the second hour someone just might black out and suffer from cirrhosis.

Some could even liken the application of drugs for what are ultimately side effects to a "band aid" effect, and you might think why we went with the dam analogy instead of the simple band aid one, since you might be wearing one right now because you didn't take our earlier advice about not saying that humans are the smartest while ravens were nearby. We didn't go for that because a band aid is actually useful. The convenient adhesive strip keeps in place the pad which seals out germs and dirt, the presence of which might prolong wound healing or even make it infected and worse. It might even have anti-bacterial properties. The point is that it accelerates the wound healing process. To call symptom treating drug use a band aid is to give band aids a bad reputation. This sort of drug application can be likened to a band aid all right, but a band aid that looks exactly like your skin where the wound is which never allows any actual healing to take place while increasing your risk of cancer on the side.

We can take a brief look at statin drugs as an example of our dam scenario, particularly because it works so well. For those unfamiliar with the statin term, it is simply a reference to the most popular type of cholesterol lowering drugs. All statins are cholesterol lowering drugs, but not all cholesterol lowering drugs are statins. Other cholesterol lowering drugs include selective cholesterol inhibitors, bile acid sequestrants, and fibrates. The names alone show that there is more than one way reduce cholesterol, but here we can focus on statins, because of the way they work.

Statin drugs hold the distinction of being the most powerful boys on the block both in terms of the power of their effects as well as their revenue. In fact, cholesterol lowering drugs in general are the cream of the crop when it comes to bringing in the bank. We could have sworn that the main purpose of drugs was supposed to be something else, but we can't quite place our fingers on it. Lipitor® was already the best-selling pharmaceutical drug in 2003, which is going on 9 years ago as of this writing. So what kind of side effects are we talking about here from statin medications?

You know, the usual. One that is always good to talk about is myopathy. Myopathy simply means muscle disease in Greek (does nobody in the medical community speak English), and can be described as muscle weakness caused by faulty function of muscle fibers. Well that sounds pretty mild, if all we have to worry about is maybe not being able to lift some weights here and there and maybe having a sore arm. The problem here is that the ol' heart is just a big muscle, and a pretty important one at that. This myopathy can affect the pumping function of the heart, a function some would say is best left unaffected.[18]

From myopathy, we can piggyback onto another more serious side effect called rhabdomyolysis. Rhabdomyolysis is the rapid breakdown of skeletal muscle cells, which can lead to serious issues. Skeletal muscle is the term for the muscle that we use to move the skeleton, which is an odd way of phrasing all the muscles that we use for locomotion. The biceps and triceps that you are using to hold up this book (or e-reader, you dastardly technophile) are an example of skeletal muscle. We don't want to go too deep into the scientific details of skeletal muscle breakdown and how it leads to dangerous complications, but suffice to say a bunch of stuff comes out that is not meant to and begins to cause some damage. Are statin drugs the only way you can potentially get rhabdomyolysis? Certainly not!

There is a plethora of things just waiting out there to damage your skeletal muscle. Some violent examples that come to mind are getting struck by lightning and receiving a crushing injury from the likes of a car accident. Other examples include heatstroke and viral infections. While the common reactions to rhabdomyolysis include bothersome things like muscle pain, weakness, confusion, and nausea, complications can arise and include the likes of an inflamed liver, irregular heartbeat, and cardiac arrest. Acute renal failure is a very dangerous complication that can happen in 15% of individuals with rhabdomyolysis.[19] This is simply another term for acute kidney failure, which has a high incidence of mortality (the overall measure of deaths in a population). We can make do without one kidney; but when both lefty and righty are taken out, the prognosis quickly becomes rather bleak.

One particular statin drug, Baycol®, was pulled from the worldwide market in 2001 because the incidence of fatal cases of rhabdomyolysis was between 16 and 80 times greater than with other statin drugs.[20] Based on all this data we can make some tentative statements. Now, we're not going to say that taking statin drugs is the same as getting struck by lightning, because that isn't a fair comparison. We're just going to note the fact that what can happen to your skeletal muscle system when you get struck by an exceptionally large bolt of electricity hotter than the surface of the sun can also potentially happen if you take an easy to swallow pill to manage your cholesterol. We always try to be optimistic that there aren't many links present between manifestations of the rage of Zeus and medical treatment.

At this point, the side effects are going to keep rolling in, so we'll make a quick list of some other ones for easy perusal.

❖ Statin therapy can be a cause of cognitive impairment (I can't think good doctor), dementia (who bought me these awful pants and what year is it), memory loss (I really hope I'm not a government assassin because I honestly can't remember), and peripheral neuropathy (my arm won't stop twitching and my nerves are hurting something fierce).[21-25]

❖ There have been documented cases of lupus-like conditions, inflammation of the lungs and chest, and joint pain without swelling.[26] If there is one type of condition that an individual likely does not want to have, it would certainly be lupus-like.

❖ The occurrence of side effects has been observed to be as high as 73.6% and 74.9% for certain statin drugs.[27]

❖ While statin drugs decrease death from heart disease by 15%, this is offset by increased deaths from cancers, gallbladder disease, and injuries.[28] As always, when we deal with an end result of death in cases and studies such as these, it tends to overshadow everything else. If 20,000 people were on statin drugs and less died from heart disease but the overall number of coffins filled was the same, they might tend to not care about how they died. Death is a somewhat serious "condition" and the end result does not become milder for the one experiencing it depending on how it happened.

❖ Higher incidences of cancer in groups using cholesterol lowering drugs has been noted, specifically in regards to gastrointestinal cancer.[29]

❖ While the advertisements would imply that a multitude of older individuals are taking cholesterol lowering drugs while going on exciting mountain biking expeditions and kayaking trips while happy as can be, well one would assume that if they're having such a great time they'll just keep taking cholesterol lowering drugs for a while. After all, those mountains aren't going to bike themselves. Studies show instances where 60% of users discontinued their medication over a period of 12 months and only one third of people on a lipid lowering regimen finish it.[30,31] Maybe those mountains are going to have to wait after all.

Certainly none of these side effects are pleasant, hence their label. But let's tie this in with our previous issue, cost and convenience. While looking through the green tint of money and how it is impacted is not the best approach to medicine by far, the exchange of goods and services does in fact run on it in the modern world. We can't give our doctors some apples in a barter exchange for a colonoscopy, because that isn't how it works anymore and we would certainly be sad about the amount of apples we would have to give up. Not to mention the fact that we are setting ourselves up for a fall by getting rid of all those apples because they contain agents that can prevent colorectal cancer.[32]

Freedom Isn't Free (Neither is Healthcare)

Let's consider cost. We've already noted how expensive angioplasties and coronary bypass procedures are each year, and the vast amount of people who get them. While the cost of each operation may seem excessive and perhaps even astronomical (or outright impossible for people who can't afford them), we must always keep in mind that surgery has an extremely large amount of factors that go into the cost. It is easy to brush off that cost as going towards our local doctor's "Ferrari Fund," but obviously this is far from the truth. The equipment, the medication, the possibly multiple doctors as well as the requisite multiple nurses, the building the operation is performed in, well we could keep going for a while. All these things can increase the cost by quite a bit because they aren't exactly cheap. Were certain most would agree that this is better than the doctor getting you drunk and cutting you open on that bit of comfortable grass in the nearby meadow.

Going away from cost to the operators, we mustn't forget the people going under the knife. While they usually pay a monthly insurance fee to cover such occurrences, not all policies are created equal and the patient might pay for the procedure from everyone's favorite money source - "out of pocket." Depending on the surgery, the patient might have to stay in the hospital for post-operative recovery and hospital room stays don't exactly go according to roadside motel nightly rates.

Last, we can never forget about the government and our most beloved friends, the insurance companies. On an individual basis, we might be unhappy with paying the health insurance each month, but we have to consider how the system works. While naturally part of the cost is devoted solely to profit (as in any business anywhere), the insurance company isn't exactly just squirreling away mountains of cash all the way to the bank. Let's say that the cost of an operation is $90,000 and is completely covered for the individual who is using the insurance, and let's say that 900 people are paying $100 a month for insurance. Obviously this example is greatly simplified in the interest of easy mathematics because let's leave the calculus to the engineers working on alternative energy sources. For the insurance company to cover this operation, it would use the money equivalent of 900 monthly payments from a group of people at a certain level of insurance, or to put in other terms the money that an individual paying the $100 rate would have paid over the course of 75 years.

How does the government play into this? This of course depends entirely of which country you are a citizen. In the United States, as always with our default example, the government has Medicare which covers about 48 million people, with the latest total population figures being about 313 million. This government run insurance system covers slightly less than 50% of all costs for individuals who have it. We would obviously modify this value greatly for countries which have a much more robust or even all inclusive public health system. The point is, such government programs are funded through taxes, which people pay as well.

Ultimately, in either case the people are paying for their health care. So what happens when instead of cheaper preventative measures, the amount of surgeries and complicated intervention slowly keeps going up? The overall cost to the people, regardless of private or public insurance, will go up. One thing to remember is that while people can grumble a good bit about paying for health insurance, they are going to complain about paying higher taxes even more.

Instead of the most expensive game of "pick your poison" ever, perhaps some common sense needs to be injected into the modern medical system. This ties in with the issue of convenience. It is much more convenient to take some lighter preventative measures instead of getting cut open by a surgeon down the line. Less surgeries and complicated medical intervention can filter down to the people paying for these things in the first place, and everyone can function a little bit better. There is even the potential for the coverage of more issues and treatments through insurance if not as much money is being thrown into the whirlpool of preventable disease management and complex intervention.

The long and short of this all is that a bigger focus on a preventative medical approach is ultimately the superior choice when it comes to these diseases. Spending can be decreased across the board, from the individual at the bottom of the contributory scale (which interestingly enough is also the part of the scale that is affected the most) to the very top at the corporation and government levels. The possibility of extending government insurance to more people or decreasing the cost of private insurance can also open up the door to the uninsured. A recent study shows that up to 45,000 working age Americans die due to being uninsured compared to their privately insured counterparts, where ideally such a number wouldn't exist either because the insurance is more affordable to the people in question or the government can help out.[33]

But most importantly, such a focus on medicine has the potential to greatly increase the quality of life for those involved. There has been a lot of mention about the certain suboptimal treatment procedures associated with conventional medicine and preventable disease, but other than the controllable environmental risk factors that were covered, there hasn't been much elucidation about alternative therapies. Well, we're about to fix that by introducing you to the key players in the hormone game, a cutthroat affair where some will overtake you by strength while others will make you bleed regularly.

While Heracles gets the *lion's share* of credit for his exploits, we can attribute much of his success to what must have been a god-like amount of testosterone. Ancient Greek secret and all that.

PART III

On the Nature and Effects of Hormones

So what's this all about hormones? We all have them, and know that those darn teenagers have perhaps too many of them, but we as a society have been conditioned for both apathy and mistrust in regard to these vital substances. If they are as important as we imply them to be, something we will show in this chapter, then why do we still suffer from those preventable diseases. If they're so powerful, why don't they counteract our smoking, our obesity, or our diabetes? Hormones do their job all too well. So what's the problem?

Time. Time is the problem. Well, not specifically time, because while the understanding of time may help us go into the far future to then flee from communist inspired underground dwelling creatures, it won't stop our hormones from going down. Time in the sense that it passes, and while it passes we are hopefully alive to see it pass, and thus we age.

Think back to that old Chevy (or Peugeot, if you are so inclined and perhaps are also French) you have sitting out in the driveway. Always you thought, man I had so much fun on that old boy, I'm definitely going to take care of it and polish it up, and I'll definitely fix the old engine up, have her purr like a kitten hittin' 100 down the freeway. But then, perhaps, the Chevy is still sitting out there, in disrepair. Maybe you've been too busy, or maybe your wife thinks that Chevy restoration money is better spent on your kid's "college education." Perhaps it's in the garage, maybe it has a tarp over it. Regardless of where it is, if you aren't keeping up with it and making sure all the internal systems are in working order and the paint is still as good as that time you went down to the levy, then that Chevy isn't exactly going to run well.

The human body is much like an automobile. In the prime of existence, both the car and yourself will have a ball, going fast and hauling lumber for your next great construction project. But, much like that old Chevy, if the human body isn't taken care of, it will go into decline. Unfortunately, while we can tune up the old car and make it run "good as new," the situation is a bit more difficult on the biological side.

We humans, as organisms, age and our overall function begins to decline. Unfortunately, we aren't possibly immortal like lobsters (a thought to keep in mind next time you go out for seafood).[1] Nor are we highly resistant to extreme heat, laugh at overwhelming radiation, sneer at atmospheric pressure higher than the depths of the ocean, and can survive in outer space like the waterbears (tardigrades). We are just humans, and while we may have invented majestic, individually sealed snack cakes, we nonetheless perish due to our mortality.

**Did you hear the one about humans trying to live in outer space?
Hah, how droll!**

Before we do ultimately perish, we go through stages of life. Before our teens, we are developing quickly and absorbing information like a sponge. Time moves slowly by because we haven't yet lived long enough to see how fast it moves in comparison to our lives, and we have boundless energy to run around on grand adventures inside haunted mansions. When the teenage years hit, puberty comes at us like the world champion at the demolition derby. Those "hormones" that we always blame for the behavior of teenagers is simply a large spurt of production tying in the transition to adult hood, which some individuals find hard to cope with, the ungrateful little curs.

Then come the roaring 20s. This decade of life is the peak of hormone production in the human lifespan, and while we spend an inordinate amount of time wondering when people are going to start calling us sir or miss, we fail to realize that this is as good as it gets internally. On average after this time period is over, the slow decline begins. We begin to notice that it is hard to get as excited about life in general, that we aren't as full of energy as we used to be, and why is that stupid alarm clock ringing already didn't we just go to sleep?

One would hope it abates at a point, but of course it gets worse. The dreaded menopause and andropause (that's right men, its coming for you as well) hit us, and life in general can be pretty rough as we try to transition from even less hormonal production. There is probably a joke in there somewhere about how **men**opause is the one that affects women, but we can thank the Greeks for ruining that (meaning cessation of month, in this case monthly cycles).

As age keeps advancing, the systems in place for the creation of hormones are impacted throughout the body. Naturally the levels cannot be maintained close to the ones in youth. The means of production and conversion degrade over time along with the rest of our body. Hormones aren't the only ones impacted either. Here is one example. The reason that many of us dislike the music kids listen to nowadays isn't simply because they have no taste in the really good stuff from back in the day but because of something that is at work in the body.

Dopamine is an important neurotransmitter (chemical created by nerve cells to send messages to other nerve cells) in our brain that is responsible for many things, one of them being our reaction to rewards or rewarding behavior. Studies show that when we listen to music that we like, even when we anticipate listening to music that we like, larger amounts of dopamine than normal are released in our brain.[2] Meanwhile, as the brain and body ages, creation of dopamine significantly decreases.[3]

Now think back to the past when you were young, while wearing your leg warmers or Members Only jacket, where you got so excited when the new Pat Benatar (or AC/DC, if you prefer) song came out. That flood of dopamine that you received when listening to your favorite music will slowly diminish over time because the overall level is diminishing as well. Ultimately, while you may like new music, that "authentic" rush that you got when you were younger is lost to the ravages of time. This is partly the reason that "they don't make music like they used to." This also means that while we can keep yelling at teenagers about hormones, they can yell back at us for our "lame" dopamine.

It doesn't have to end with music either. We simply brought it up because it is an easily associated thing that happens with age. Perhaps they "don't make ice cream like they used to." Maybe even you miss the cafeteria food from school in the 1950s, despite the Hepatitis A you got from that place. Pleasurable experiences can decline with age due to the decreased amount of dopamine that you have in the old noggin. Going forward, keep this in mind and put into context with any hormone that we will be looking at in depth. Maybe math is a little harder now, the old running legs aren't doing a lot of running nowadays, and so on. But let's not get too far ahead of ourselves - what exactly are hormones in the first place?

The Couriers of Life

Basically, a hormone is a chemical that acts as a messenger, manufactured by a cell to be transported to another cell. While this pre-requisite naturally excludes any single celled organisms due to the nature of such an action, all multi-cellular organisms contain hormones. Even the grass outside of your house is creating plant hormones when it isn't wondering when the next time you will mow it or get rid of all those freeloading dandelions that moved in.

The actual word hormone is based from the Greek word for "impetus," which the dictionary defines as "driving force, impulse, or stimulus." This is quite the apt description for the ridiculous range of abilities and influences that hormones have, but especially so as the description of the driving force for so many things. Small quantities of hormones can have a great effect on cellular metabolism, cracking the whip so to speak and getting everything in gear. After hormones reach a target cell, they bind to receptors either inside the cell or within the cell membrane, after which the cellular response is initiated.

The endocrine glands in the body have the job of main hormone production and release hormones directly into the bloodstream to their target destinations. Major endocrine glands are the pineal gland, the pituitary gland, the thyroid gland, the adrenal gland, the pancreas, and the gonads (ovaries in females and testes in males). The hormones created from these glands will fuel the upcoming discussion and feature the prominent part in the restorative medicine approach.

Hormones themselves can be broken up into two different categories based on their chemical makeup. Peptide hormones are formed from chains of amino acids and include such staples as insulin, growth hormone, and prolactin. Lipid and phospholipid hormones are derived from lipids and include the steroid hormones, which include the familiar heavyweights such as testosterone and estrogens.

While we are on the subject of chemical messengers, we will also include an observation of monoamines. These potent neurotransmitters include key players such as melatonin, serotonin, and the previously mentioned dopamine. These chemicals should most certainly be considered when we consider a restorative approach to medicine. After all, it would be nice if we could come to appreciate that hullabaloo that our children call "sweet tunes" and maybe vanilla ice cream will once again taste like true vanilla ice cream by Jove! For now, we focus on the heavy artillery, the steroid hormones.

Simplified Chain of Steroid Hormone Production and Conversion

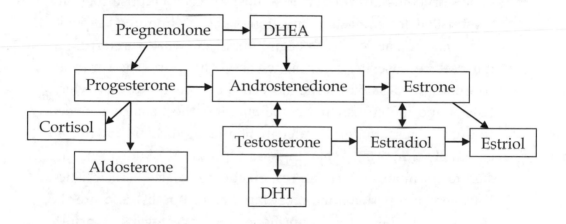

In this instance, the arrows represent the route of conversion, where one hormone turns into another. What is important to note about this flow chart, other than the fact it looks like a spider web constructed by an arachnid under the influence of caffeine, is that much like the name implies, it is extremely simplified. For example, between pregnenolone and DHEA (Dehydroepiandrosterone, which is why nobody is writing that one out each time we mention it), there is an intermediate in the link by the name of 17αhydroxypregnenolone. Another example is that progesterone does not convert directly into cortisol, but must first become 11-deoxycorticosterone, then corticosterone, and then cortisol. We are also neglecting to mention the actual enzymes that carry out these conversion steps because we don't want to fill your head with names like 3β-hydroxysteroid dehydrogenase (science, why are you so complicated) when what we want to focus on are the actual steroid hormones.

We can group steroid hormones into five groups due to the receptors to which they bind. The groups are glucocorticoids, mineralocorticoids, androgens, estrogens, and progestogens. Glucocorticoids are present in almost all cells because they are responsible for important functions such as immune response and metabolic activity. The beginning of the word is referring to glucose, because these hormones serve to keep blood glucose concentrations stable. Mineralocorticoids are hormones which have important functions in maintaining the balance between sodium, potassium, and water, which leads to them having an extremely important role in blood pressure. Androgens are steroid hormones which are responsible for male characteristics. Estrogens are perhaps the most familiar in this list and are the primary female sex hormones. Progestogens include progesterone, which plays important roles in both pregnancy and the menstrual cycle, among many others, but is also present in men in smaller quantities.

That last bit might confuse some people. After all, men are manly men and getting pregnant certainly isn't on the list of some burly lumberjack. He is concerned with chopping down the forest, not conceiving a child. Also, he has no uterus. This is where the label of "female" and "male" hormones sticks out like a sore thumb. Both sexes have the hormones, it is only a matter of differing qualities. Testosterone, the "manly" hormone that drives men to fell trees and burn up the dance floor in elaborate courtship rituals, is also present in women in much smaller quantities. However, as we will point out later, even though women might have a small level of testosterone overall, it does not mean that a decrease in this small level can't have sizeable impacts in certain areas. Now that we've covered a bit of the background behind the hormones, we can look at the actual hormones that play a large role in our approach to restorative medicine. This is meant as a showcase for the power and potential hormones, with more digestible lists of symptoms and issues available in the next chapter for easy reference.

Pregnenolone, the Grandfather of All

There goes that gender based hormonal language again. We could have called pregnenolone the grandmother of all, but then we don't win either. Perhaps we can refer to pregnenolone as the grandparent of all. So, pregnenolone, the ~~grandfather~~ grandparent of all, is the steroid hormone seen previously in the chart which is the point of origin for conversion for the others, hence the moniker we have given it. While pregnenolone is not a household name, it is nonetheless a very important hormone that seems to be ignored in public discourse relating to all things hormonal. Which is a shame really, not to mention a horrifically grave oversight.

Pregnenolone is also the first hormone that we will be looking at that is also belongs not only to the steroid hormone family, but also to the neuroactive steroid classification. For simplicity's sake, these are often called neurosteroids. Neurosteroids are key players in the inner workings of the nervous system because they can influence the excitability of neurons.[4] On the whole, neurons tend to be quite an excitable bunch. When neurons communicate, they shoot out messages both through chemicals and electricity. While this does not unfortunately give us lightning based magic or super powers, it does mean that on the whole, impulses and messages travel along your nervous system at breakneck speeds.

For example, move your arm up and down. You didn't just think - ok time to move my arm, ok I am starting to flex these muscles to raise my arm up and down, and hooray, I am now moving my arm up and down. Of course that's not how it happened. You read the words, you moved your arm, and all is good in the world because you didn't have to think, you just did it. But of course our neurons are not simply made for us to move our arm around while trying to figure out the inner workings of such an action, but are also responsible for our daily functions that enable us to live. It's easy, then, to see how hormones, which are already entrenched on the cellular level like guerrillas in the mountain or a bad rash, that affect the nervous system are even more important than we give them credit for. We can't neglect to reiterate that neurosteroids **control** excitability and do not simply **excite**. Being able to respond to stimuli in a timely fashion and reacting to impulses quickly is very important, but being able to tone down and "chill out" is just as important.

What about pregnenolone and the nerves then? Are we just content to say that as a neurosteroid it is exceptionally good for you to have for a well-oiled nervous system? Certainly not. We can look at specific instances where the presence or lack thereof of pregnenolone ties in well with its function as a neurosteroid. We must never forget that while we can attribute the noun "nerves" to a lot of concepts tangible and intangible, the

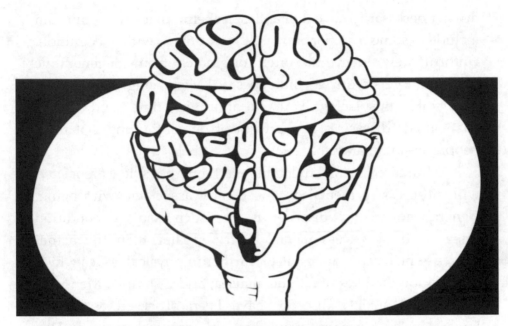

control center of our bodies is the brain and is composed of a staggering amount of neurons (certainly more than 80 billion of them).[5] While impaired nerves around the body can lead to milder things like the occasional twitch or slowed reflex, impaired neural activity in the brain can lead to some serious mental impairments.

Elderly patients with dementia have been observed as having low pregnenolone levels.[6] While many of us might be familiar with the term, in practical application the word dementia may be even a little watered down in popular perception. Dementia is the decrease in mental function that is outside the realm of normal aging. Think of it as the difference between grandpa misplacing his book and then remembering that he left it out on the veranda or permanently forgetting where he buried that chest of gold that is to be your inheritance (in which case we would also assume that your grandpa forgot to tell you about his scurvy fighting days as a pirate). Dementia doesn't necessarily have to manifest as being that severe, and can include some minor overall trouble with cognition. Unfortunately, dementia often originates from degenerative issues and gets worse as time goes on. Misplacing the keys can turn into misplacing your location in time and space. Alzheimer's disease is also a form of dementia, one that most people are familiar with.

Impaired mental function is certainly not solely associated with progressive mental decline greatly associated with aging. Generalized anxiety disorder is one such issue, a condition categorized by excess mental worry greater than the actual source, which can manifest itself further in physical issues which can include the likes of fatigue, nausea, and insomnia. Men with generalized anxiety disorder have been observed as having lower levels of pregnenolone than their control groups.[7] This condition is the most common disorder in the workplace and is highly debilitating, with a high co-frequency of depression and other anxiety issues.[8] Margin trading stock brokers and employees of corporations who don't "believe in raises" can most probably relate.

A lack of pregnenolone has also been seen in individuals suffering from good old fashioned depression as well.[9] Nobody really needs an introduction to depression, since everyone has almost certainly been afflicted by it at some point or another. While the natural reaction is to disagree, we have to remember that depression is the catch all for all manner of depressive issues. It can be of the mild transient variety, like the time a crack commando squad of strawberry bud weevils infiltrated your potted garden on the terrace and destroyed your crop, or it can be of the severe "clinical depression" variety, the one with serious issues such as insomnia or suicidal thoughts after an ex-girlfriend burned our first edition printing of Harry Potter. What we can say as a blanket statement is that depression is the wide range of depressed or low mood. At this point pregnenolone has asked us to mention that it is also a player in mood control itself.[10]

Supplementation of pregnenolone has been shown to improve the body's response to stress.[11] Someone should probably tell that to those generalized anxiety guys. Pregnenolone also has indications for benefits in areas such as arthritis, immune system function, and heart health. An important thing to remember is that we don't throw the title of grandparent to pregnenolone lightly. Conversion plays a large role in the creation of steroid hormone production, and if there is not enough pregnenolone to go around and convert into the next steps, then other areas will naturally suffer as well. To an extent, we can see the implication that a deficiency in the previous "tier" of hormones can cause a deficiency in the current tier as well. If we're running a tin can producing operation and start to run low on tin, then things are going to get hairy real fast.

DHEA, Ambiguously Manly

When we speak about DHEA, we usually go the quick and steady route of thinking that it is some kind of powerhouse that can push us to great feats of strength and endurance. This wouldn't be too far from the mark. After all, we hear all about how the testing committee in charge of ferreting out dopers and steroid users at the Olympic Games bans DHEA. So how about the link between DHEA and all things physical?

First, we have to note that DHEA binds to androgen receptors, thus already giving it "street cred" in regards to its interaction with the physical realm. As we mentioned earlier, androgens are the "male" hormones and have a close link with such activity. In fact, exercising regularly has been shown to increase DHEA levels.[12] DHEA also happens to be the most proliferated steroid hormone in the body.[13] When we speak about DHEA levels, one of two values is usually used: DHEA and DHEA-Sulfate (DHEA-S). DHEA-S is a metabolite of DHEA and can actually convert back into its precursor. The thing with DHEA-S is that much more of it can be found in the blood, which consequently provides a better gauge of how much DHEA is currently in the body. For this reason, the value of DHEA-S is more often used for accurate readings.

DHEA is made primarily in the adrenal glands, with other locations of production including the testes and brain.[14,15] One might point out to testes as being a male only occurrence, and we would tend to agree. However, as far as androgens go, testosterone is the one that has a much greater ratio in men than in women, whereas in DHEA sulfate the difference is certainly there, but not as pronounced. After all, women being of the human species have adrenal glands and brains just as men do (though some women might object about the latter for some specimens).

While we want to shy away from going into deep detail about the glands that are responsible for hormone production because our focus is on the steroid hormones themselves, we can look at the adrenal cortex for a specific example in its interaction with DHEA. The adrenal gland is certainly not limited to the production of just androgens, but also the glucocorticoids, mineralocorticoids, and corticosteroids. The gland is made up of two parts, the cortex and medulla, and the cortex can be seen as consisting of layers, where the various hormones are produced. DHEA in particular is created in the innermost layer, the zona reticularis (you can purge this name from your memory, because there's no test at the end and it isn't a very interesting factoid to drop at your next cocktail party). Decreased levels of DHEA in the body can lead to atrophy of this area.[16] Words that most people don't wish to hear in conjunction with major organs do include atrophy.

We mentioned earlier with pregnenolone the concept of decreased production tiers with steroid hormone interconversion. With DHEA in particular, we can easily see this in action. We already know that decreasing hormone levels due to breakdown of function is central to aging. When we talk about DHEA level decreases due to age, we notice that as this level gets smaller, the production of androgens can decrease by half.[17] Let's shoot through the list of androgens again - DHEA, androstenedione, androstenediol, androsterone, testosterone, and dihydrotestosterone (DHT). If you look back at the chart in the beginning of the chapter, some of those are not present due to the simplification process. However, if you follow full, non-simplified pathways down, all of the others originate from DHEA. If we observe a specific decade of life and compared it to the optimal, mainly being the 50-60 year old range as compared to the 20-30 year old range, then we can see that DHEA levels decrease by 74% in men and by 70% in women.[18]

Another interesting action that happens to discredit the concept of androgens as being male hormones even further is what happens to women post menopause. After the dreaded event occurs, almost all estrogens created in women are produced from conversion via DHEA. Even before menopause, this number can be as high as 70%. So here we have DHEA, which is a "male" hormone, contributing in extremely large quantities to the most prominent "female" hormone. This is why gender labels for steroid hormones are bad, no matter how convenient they are, because they give people a wrong interpretation of hormones when they first learn about them as well as a lingering preconceived notions about hormones that are of the "opposite gender." One would certainly not expect DHEA supplementation to aid older women in getting pregnant, but it does.[19] In fact, DHEA supplementation is used all around as an additional therapy when treating female infertility.[20]

We spent a good amount earlier covering how heart disease is a major killer and DHEA is certainly no slouch in this department. Higher levels of DHEA-S have an association with better survival in cases of cardiovascular disease.[21] DHEA is classified as a neurosteroid, just like pregnenolone, and has a variety of associated benefits, in particular when speaking about taking DHEA to improve levels. DHEA supplementation can cause improvements in memory, mood, and even chronic depression.[22,23] When older individuals suffering from major depression and low DHEA-S levels were given DHEA supplementation to bring up their levels to more youthful ones, both their depression and memory improved in conjunction with the increased levels of DHEA-S and DHEA (don't forget that these can convert into each other). [24]

But that's enough about one all around powerhouse, because we have more to cover. In the interest of knocking out androgens quickly so we can move on to the "female" hormones, we will be looking at testosterone next.

Testosterone, the Lumberjack Hormone

Testosterone, then, the mighty male hormone. The testosterone that starts fisticuffs and fights wars. The testosterone that makes men build large objects that most certainly are not any form of compensation. The testosterone that is produced in the ovaries. Wait, that last one seems a bit off. But of course, you are well aware of our ploy to discredit gender labels on hormones at this point. Of course testosterone is produced in the ovaries, because women don't have testes (which are the main production area in men, to the surprise of absolutely nobody).

After some snickering reminiscent of the sexual education classroom in middle school, a time period awkward for everybody, one naturally wants to tie in libido and sexual drive with testosterone. After all, with the testes and ovaries and whatnot, it would make sense and would certainly be correct. The function of the aforementioned organs is meant to propagate the species, so it is certainly natural that a hormone produced there would play a large part in the act.

Naturally, we wouldn't be liable to call testosterone the lumberjack hormone if we didn't put in a comment somewhere about morning wood. There is a clear link between testosterone levels and male "potency", as well as a strong link between low levels of testosterone and erectile dysfunction. Men who received testosterone supplementation had improved sexual function.[25] Going based on our previous mention that ovaries produce testosterone in women, it makes sense that testosterone supplementation helped improve sexual function in women suffering from sexual dysfunction.[26]

We have been putting a lot of focus on dispelling the myth of male hormone specificity, but what about the things that gave androgens and testosterone in specific such a male focused leaning? A large part of it has to do with the final stages of male development before the full transition into adulthood. These final developmental stages include the maturation of bone growth, increase in body and facial hair, and increased muscle mass and strength. In short, everything that begins to define the human male as a full adult man. This can certainly cross over into the female realm as well.

The female breast, for example, is composed in large part of adipose tissue, which in turn is mostly fat (but not fully). Estrogens play a role in the development of breasts, which is largely negated in men due to their high testosterone levels (in part due to the fact that testosterone helps prevent fat accumulation). However, in the example of female bodybuilders on the extreme end of professional competition category, the breasts as visible anatomical entities begin to greatly decline as muscle mass is increased in great proportion and overall body fat is decreased. Granted, these are extreme cases that are frequently associated with pharmaceutical approaches to increasing testosterone levels, but it does show that to look like a man one does not necessarily have to be a man. Even the anatomic feature colloquially known as "man jaw" can arise, which is also aided by testosterone's role in decreasing fat layers deep beneath the skin in the human face.

It seems clear that testosterone plays a large part in muscle growth and health and certainly we can't forget about the muscle in our chest beating an average of 70 times per minute. In one particular study, men who suffered from coronary artery disease had a correlation between low testosterone values and decreased survival.[27] Such studies on the nature of heart disease and testosterone are mainly centered around men, because even the scientific approach is not immune to gender labeling of hormones. In one study made only on women with chronic heart failure, testosterone supplementation was seen as a potential treatment option.[28]

Does that wrap it up in the coverage of testosterone? Not quite. It seems that testosterone, when it isn't responsible for defending ancient Greece from a Persian invasion, has a knack for making the brain work well. Supplementation of testosterone has been shown to help improve neurons suffering from inadequate function. We're sure that the neurons just had a long day at work and are too tired to work properly at that particular time. People who have Lou Gehrig's disease have been observed as having lower levels of testosterone.[29] Unfortunately, this disease (amyotrophic lateral sclerosis), does not turn a person into a baseball powerhouse, but instead causes deterioration of motor neurons (the neurons that control voluntary movement in the body) which is followed by death primarily from respiratory failure.

Estrogens, the Many as One

Those in the know might immediately recognize the plural of everyone's favorite female hormone, but others might be confused why its estrogens and not estrogen. Also, these people clearly skipped over the beginning of this chapter where there was no "estrogen" in the flow chart. While there are many estrogens circulating out and about, the primary players are estrone (E1), estradiol (E2), and estriol (E3). In this instance we use the term key players not to describe notoriety but through actual circulating amount - these three combined make up the bulk of estrogens in the body.

Because estrogens can be seen as the natural opposite of testosterone, their function in the development of the female body goes without saying. Estrogens are indeed responsible for the maturation of female secondary sex characteristics such as breast development, widening of hips, and accumulation of fat in certain areas. Estrogens also most certainly play a large role in the function of the female reproductive system. But again, we cannot fall into the gender hormone trap and must mention that estrogen actually has an important role in male reproduction. Estradiol in particular helps prevent the apoptosis (programmed cell death) of sperm cells.[30] Remember men, next time you successfully help make a baby because not too many of your soldiers died off in the interim, you can thank estradiol.

Fluctuating levels of estrogens and progesterone help keep the monthly cycles regular. The concept of balance between estrogen and progesterone is something we will cover when we introduce the latter. During the regular 28 day monthly cycle of menstruation, estrogen goes up to peak levels towards the middle of this time frame in conjunction with ovulation (the process of egg release), and then drops off and hits the lowest amount prior and during menstruation, to repeat the process again until the cycle breaks with the onset of menopause.

The link between estrogen and bone health is perhaps a more subtle one. At the rate that we see commercials on television about osteoporosis that focus entirely on women, we might as well have men high-fiving each other in the background while complimenting each other on their robust skeletal architecture. Osteoporosis hardly needs an introduction, being a well-known disease that decreases bone mineral density which makes the bones more liable to break. Another prominent fact is that the best state to have bones in is the unbroken state. But we all know about great-grandma's walker with the tennis balls cut in half on the bottom, but we might not know particularly that bones are constantly broken down for parts (to put it crudely) and reformed. What happens during osteoporosis is that this normally healthy ratio of breakdown and creation is tilted toward the destructive process. Lower levels of estrogens load the dice in favor of the break down process, levels which plummet like the stock market on Black Tuesday.

Bones and reproduction aside, meant entirely non-metaphorically, we can't let the estrogens get away without mentioning the beneficial effect it can have on our old friends the neurons. At this rate you might think of course it has an impact on neural activity, what steroid hormone doesn't? We would tend to agree with that. Estrogen therapy during and post menopause seem to fare very well when braving the turbulent waters of impending Alzheimer's disease.[31] Restoration of estrogens to optimal levels helps women recover from depressions after child birth, during the process of menopause, and post menopause.[32] When women are afflicted with such types of depression, the public branding is to call them "hormonal," whereas a title that rings more true would be "big old lack of hormonal."

Progesterone, the Great Stabilizer

Progesterone gets a bit of a diminished reputation, and unfairly so, because a large part of its efforts seem to be aimed at helping balance out against estrogen. This is definitely true, as far as major functions of progesterone go. But if we have learned anything so far, it is that no hormone operates solely based on the assumptions that people have about them. While we're speaking of the mediating properties of progesterone, we should cover an important aspect that is a major part in the restorative medical approach when it comes to these two "female" hormones.

Progesterone fluctuates based on the monthly cycle just as estrogen does. Unlike estrogen, progesterone gradually increases and then spikes in the later part of the cycle. However, it does drop off drastically like estrogen just prior to menstruation. The regular cycle is part of the monthly balancing act, but a much larger balancing game is afoot in overall levels. Premenstrual syndrome, the scourge of women everywhere and better known as PMS, is related to the fluctuations of progesterone. This brings up the concept of estrogen dominance or progesterone dominance.

We must stress the dominance part of this terminology. The term dominant does not specifically mean large or high in the grand scheme of things. For example, let's say that in a local area, a group of cotton farmers all had their crop output horribly maimed by a plague worthy infestation of boll weevils (weevils that eat cotton buds and flowers). One of these farmers turns out with the dominant amount of production in his cotton crop, but since everyone's output is greatly diminished, this "domination" works around small numbers. Meanwhile on a good year with bumper crops, if that same farmer has the most production he will dominate again, but with high levels all around the board. Regardless of the overall levels, dominant simply means the highest in that group, regardless of the group size.

This is the exact same concept at work here, except we have progesterone and estrogens which work with each other. But then there's a whole different matter of ratios going on. There are issues associated with low progesterone and/or estrogens, as well as with high progesterone and/or estrogens. But then, there are also issues associated with dominance of progesterone or estrogens. So let's say a woman has a low level of progesterone and a high level of estrogens. She would get issues associated with a low level of progesterone, potential issues associated with high estrogen, and then to sweeten the unsavory pot issues associated with estrogen dominance (though in this case the issues of estrogen dominance would likely overshadow issues of high estrogen). Take the same woman and make the estrogens level lower than the progesterone, and she would have issues associated with low progesterone, low estrogen, and progesterone dominance. The level of progesterone in women tends to decline faster with age than that of estrogen, which means that this particular age related decline favors the condition of estrogen dominance rather than progesterone dominance. Like all processes in the body with many variables, this is not always iron clad but is mostly the case. We will knock out a proper list for easy reference associated with these when we take a closer look at the restorative approach.

Neurons are never disappointed when progesterone is around, because it can provide a benefit to mental function and can calm the nervous system. Observations have been made where women who had Parkinson's disease had fluctuating symptoms based on what stage of their menstrual cycle they were in and notable differences in pregnant women.[33] Progesterone plays a very important role in allowing women to get pregnant and carry out to full term, with very high increases in progesterone levels. Progesterone supplementation can improve the outcome of brain and central nervous system injuries through limitation of damage, decrease of nerve tissue loss, and improved recovery time.[34] One might say that all of those are more than just a bit beneficial when dealing with recovery from injuries of this sort.

We certainly couldn't let the last "female" hormone go without seeing how it specifically affects men, a tradition of sorts at this point. Much like estradiol, progesterone steps up to the plate by assisting in male reproductive efficacy. While estradiol helps prevent the death of the soldiers marching on, progesterone plays a role in actually creating them.[35] Don't get us wrong, too much estrogens in the male body isn't a great thing and can lead to some negative effects, but all things in moderation, as they say. No man can say "I'm a man, boy, and I ain't got none of them female hormones in my body," because yes, they do. If anything a crude locker room jab at a man having trouble creating children can go something along the line of "Hah, I bet that guy's progesterone and estrogen are in the dumps."

Cortisol, Stockbroker's Delight

The first impression that many people get when they hear the word cortisol is "that cream I put on my rash," but of course it wouldn't be in this section if it wasn't naturally produced in your body (also the common cream in reference here is referred to as hydrocortisone). Cortisol is frequently referred to as the stress hormone because levels are increased when the body is under stress, which also makes it the self-explanatory labeled hormone. We would say we are happy to come up to another steroid hormone that is "gender neutral," but now we have to deal with the "stress hormone" label. This is certainly an apt description of its well-known association, but sells short the variability of functions that cortisol is part of. The "establishment" just keeps on putting labels on everything.

Cortisol is produced in the cortex of the adrenal gland, in a layer more outward than the inner one that produces DHEA. Other than the stress response, there are certain functions that cortisol plays a role in. It helps with the regulation of blood pressure and cardiovascular function, helps control metabolic activity and with the breakdown of fats, carbohydrates, and proteins, and it helps suppress the immune system. Now, on the one hand such a function might seem to do more harm than good (or no good, for that matter), but we have to consider all the factors.

The human immune system is very loyal to us and efficient, but one might say it isn't too bright and can sometimes go off the deep end. Inflammation in the body is actually the response of the immune system trying to "right wrongs," as it were. However, sometimes the immune response is a bit too zealous in the approach to protecting the body, where the benefits of a moderating agent become readily apparent. Cortisol isn't trying to make you become sick easier, it's trying to reign in overeager employees in the human body.

Cortisol, like progesterone and estrogen in women, is a fluctuating hormone (in both genders). Instead of a monthly cycle, it has a daily cycle with the highest amounts present in the morning. What's important to differentiate when symptoms of high or low cortisol are discussed is the context of long term levels. One does not simply get the issues associated with low or high cortisol due to the daily fluctuations. When high and low cortisol are referred to, this is regarding high or low prolonged levels of cortisol in the blood. For example hair loss is an issue of chronic high cortisol levels, not an issue when cortisol is high in the morning.

Now that we've covered the important steroid hormones, we can move on to our approach - the restorative...approach.

Optimized physiologic function is akin to Asclepius bringing in the really good healing. Nine out of ten Greek doctors agree.

PART IV

On the Nature of the Restorative Approach

So we spent some time going over some fundamentals about the body and medicine, but where does our particular approach of "restorative medicine" fit in to this? We're glad you asked (after reading that question). The main concept to remember here is that while we showed some problematic areas with conventional medicine earlier, by no means do we eschew conventional medicine because despite any shortcomings it is so widespread because it works in so many ways, as we explained earlier.

The second is that this approach to restorative medicine only works because we co-operate with conventional, fully licensed and accredited doctors. There isn't a cadre of hedge wizards and nutritionist working on creating this approach based on what the latest popular alternative health fad is or what "breakthrough" supplement the health magazines are trying to push. Instead, a rigorous, scientific approach is made towards observable variables, existing medical literature, and a comprehensive look at how the body works and how it fails. This approach is made solely while under the overseeing eyes of physicians of the licensed kind. So how does it begin?

Individuals wishing to partake must first fill out a detailed health history of past and current issues and symptoms. This inquiry is very detailed in the areas that we approach and is fully examined. Minute details that may not mean much to the layperson can divulge a lot of information to the trained eye. However, an approach focused solely on written accounts of symptoms and issues can certainly tell us a lot, but it isn't exactly the best way to create a program. What's the best way to assess the condition of someone in a particular area? A test! In this case, a blood test.

The blood test is extremely important because while the knowledge is available to discern symptoms and descriptions of issues, actual data obtained from a blood test will help paint a much clearer picture of what is going on with regards to a suboptimal physiology. The tests that are looked at are as follows:

- ❖ **Lipid Profile**
- ❖ **Complete Blood Count (CBC)**
- ❖ **Comprehensive Metabolic Panel (CMP)**
- ❖ **Pregnenolone**
- ❖ **DHEA-Sulfate**
- ❖ **Total Testosterone**
- ❖ **Progesterone**
- ❖ **Total Estrogen**
- ❖ **Cortisol**
- ❖ **Thyroid Stimulating Hormone (TSH)**
- ❖ **Total Triiodothyronine (T3)**
- ❖ **Total Thyroxine (T4)**
- ❖ **Prolactin**
- ❖ **Serotonin**
- ❖ **25-Hydroxy Vitamin D**
- ❖ **C-Reactive Protein**
- ❖ **Homocysteine**
- ❖ **Prostate Specific Antigen (PSA)**
- ❖ **Insulin-like Growth Factor (IGF-1)**
- ❖ **Aldosterone**

Using the data gleamed from these blood tests, a physician approved program is created that consists of bio-identical hormones, supplements, and vitamins. This assembled product is individually created for each person because, believe it or not, each person's body is individualized. To find two individuals of the same age and gender having the exact same blood test results is an aberration of untold rarity and from a practical and logical approach will never be observed across the board. Granted, if someone orchestrates a plan so that all roughly 7 billion humans on the planet to take a blood test and put that data into a computer network, we might find some. Until then, we'll just repeat that for optimal results a blanket approach cannot be used.

People who are on medications stay on their medications but over time they may find that they do not need them anymore because of improved symptoms and with doctor approval and guidance can potentially discontinue them. This is especially true of cholesterol lowering medications, because this approach to restoration of function normalizes cholesterol levels naturally (we'll get to that in a bit). Other examples include drugs for depression, insomnia, and erectile dysfunction (among many others).

Other than the individualized approach to program creation, the most important part of a successful program is constant feedback from the individual. People following our approach can login to an internet system (or call in Alexander Graham Bell fashion) to provide updates as frequently as needed to receive responses or program adjustments. This is in contrast to seeing a doctor and then seeing her again in a month or more, depending on how busy the office is. The program is created in a tiered and modulated fashion so that any single item can be modified independently of others, which is partly the reason we stay away from multi-formula compounds like nobles from the peasant's quarter during a plague outbreak.

Another reason is that on regular intervals, be they 3 month or 6 month, we ask for a follow up blood test to see what effect the program is having on the various levels (other than the effects that are already noted through frequent updates in the form of symptoms). Once these tests are received, the program is almost always modified because even with a vast amount of experience in creating individualized programs based on the many factors required prior to creation, the rate at which an individual's body absorbs the agents or gets kick started into creating its own is always variable because no two people have the same increases. The full explanation of the second reason is that if a multi-formula compound approach was used, this program adjustment and program adjustments in general would quickly become an exercise in futility.

Let's say that two systems are used, one with compounded agents and one with only single agents. The patient updates the doctor with an issue or a blood test result. In both cases the doctor would say, this is the likely cause, let's modify this amount and see if the issue improves. The doctor using the single compound will be able to fix it up right as rain, but the doctor using a compounded agent will be up that certain proverbial creek with no paddle. A modification cannot be made without changing the entire compounded agent, which becomes an immense hassle and an extreme money waster. If there is one thing that's worse than a hassle, then that is a hassle that makes us spend more money.

To sum up: observations and descriptions of symptoms are assessed along with blood test results to create an individualized program under the guidance and control of a licensed physician that is then adjusted as needed based on feedback provided by the user and regular follow up blood testing. There are likely questions still on your mind such as what are all those tests for, isn't taking hormones dangerous, and what exactly constitutes the items on the program? We can begin with some brief test explanations while also covering some of the symptoms associated with hormonal deficiencies.

The Vampire's Favorite Tests

Lipid Profile - Odds are that many people are familiar with this blood test, since it comes standard on many blood requisition forms. This is simply a measure of total cholesterol, low density lipoproteins (LDL), high density lipoproteins (HDL), and triglycerides. Obviously this is public enemy number one right now, and is addressed by the restorative approach to medicine. We will go much further in detail about cholesterol in the next chapter.

Complete Blood Count (CBC) - This is the complete, but can also be called comprehensive, blood test of your blood. While that sounds awkward, it is also self-explanatory. While all the other tests are measuring specifically for certain particles floating about the blood, this test measures the components of blood itself. We can roughly describe this as a measure of the red blood cells, the white blood cells, and the platelets and their subcategories. For example in the realm of the red blood cells, the testing includes checking hemoglobin, to assess the oxygen carrying capacity of the blood and to check for conditions such as anemia, while also checking for things such as the average width of red blood cells. As many learned in high school biology, white blood cells are the defenders of the body, and naturally their subcategories relate to such events if elevated. A simple example is eosinophil granulocytes, which can point to a possible parasitic infestation, asthma, or allergic reaction. Platelets are platelets, and this test can describe how "thin" the blood is, in this sense thin referring to how readily the clotting capacity of the blood.

Comprehensive Metabolic Panel (CMP) - This test, along with the 2 above, probably rounds up the usual ones that are familiar to most people since they are part of the "regular physical" that usually happens every year. Basically, it can be separated into categories. Glucose and calcium stand in their own group, being levels of said molecules. Electrolytes include mainstays like sodium and potassium, which are certainly best served balanced. The other tests variably check on function of the kidneys and liver. The compounds in these groups naturally elevate when certain functions of the mentioned organs are impaired, and can be simple to check for indicators that something is wrong in these areas.

Pregnenolone - We covered the grandparent of the other steroid hormones previously and would simply like to repeat that while pregnenolone is not well known, its functions and impact on other hormone levels cannot be underestimated.

- ❖ Precursor of many other hormones
- ❖ Fights the effects of fatigue and stress
- ❖ Relieves arthritis pain
- ❖ Improves heart health
- ❖ Boosts the immune system
- ❖ Protects against coronary artery disease
- ❖ Improves mood and memory
- ❖ Vital for full brain function
- ❖ Protection against degenerative brain diseases

DHEA-Sulfate - As you might recall from before, this is simply a metabolite of DHEA that can convert back into it, but is the better indicator of DHEA values floating about in the blood.

❖ Improves heart health
❖ Slows the onset or progression of diabetes
❖ Has beneficial impact on arthritis
❖ Reverses declining cognitive function
❖ Low levels associated with increased risk of breast, ovarian, and other site cancer
❖ Optimal levels are associated with maximum immunity and metabolic efficiency
❖ Around 50% of total androgens in men are converted from DHEA
❖ Contributes to 70% of estrogens pre menopause and almost 100% post
❖ Levels decreased by 95% in many people by age 75 from peak levels

Total Testosterone - This is simply the total amount of testosterone in the blood. This particular test is used because the free testosterone levels are not as reliable for interpretation (you could have a high level of free testosterone but a low level of overall testosterone).

❖ Boosts the male and female libido
❖ Promotes heart health
❖ Helps prevent osteoporosis (in larger part in men)
❖ Increases muscle strength
❖ Helps control blood sugar
❖ Helps with mental concentration and improves mood
❖ Protects the brain against Alzheimer's disease

Symptoms of Low Testosterone

- ❖ Prolonged fatigue
- ❖ Memory issues
- ❖ Decreased libido
- ❖ Vaginal dryness
- ❖ Muscle weakness
- ❖ Heart palpitations
- ❖ Bone loss
- ❖ Incontinence
- ❖ Fibromyalgia
- ❖ Irritability or moodiness
- ❖ Mental fuzz
- ❖ Depression
- ❖ Decreased Motivation
- ❖ Diminished feeling of well being
- ❖ Poor self-esteem
- ❖ Thinning skin
- ❖ General aches and pains
- ❖ Insomnia
- ❖ More aggressive prostate cancer
- ❖ Loss of scalp hair

Symptoms of Low Androgens

- ❖ Emotionality
- ❖ Extra sensitivity to emotional and physical stress
- ❖ Poor self-esteem
- ❖ Poor stamina
- ❖ Poor sex drive
- ❖ Cardiovascular disease
- ❖ Osteoporosis

Progesterone - The test of the namesake. In the majority of menopausal women these values are extremely low.

- ❖ Stimulates urine production
- ❖ Calms down the central nervous system
- ❖ A natural antidepressant and tranquilizer
- ❖ Improves female libido
- ❖ Protects against cancer
- ❖ Boosts thyroid action
- ❖ Helps use rather than store body fat
- ❖ Helps prevent osteoporosis

Symptoms of Low Progesterone

- ❖ Infertility
- ❖ Thyroid dysfunction
- ❖ Depression
- ❖ Fibrocystic breasts
- ❖ Weight gain
- ❖ Gallbladder disease
- ❖ Low blood sugar
- ❖ Panic attacks
- ❖ Water retention
- ❖ Irregular menstrual cycle
- ❖ Blood clots during menstruation
- ❖ Magnesium deficiency
- ❖ Vaginal dryness
- ❖ Breast tenderness
- ❖ Painful and swollen breasts
- ❖ Swollen extremities (prior to menses)
- ❖ Excessive menstruation
- ❖ Premenstrual syndrome
- ❖ Cysts and cancers of the breasts and ovaries
- ❖ Fibroids and uterine cancer

Symptoms of Progesterone Deficiency

- ❖ Irregular menses
- ❖ Heavy bleeding
- ❖ Cramping
- ❖ Swollen breasts
- ❖ Low libido
- ❖ Excess emotionality
- ❖ Excess sensitivity
- ❖ Depression and nervousness
- ❖ Anxiety and irritability
- ❖ Mood swings
- ❖ Weight gain
- ❖ Restless sleep
- ❖ Headaches
- ❖ Premenstrual migraine
- ❖ Acne
- ❖ Premenstrual syndrome
- ❖ Mental fuzz
- ❖ Joint pain

Symptoms of Progesterone Dominance and Excess

- ❖ Swelling of breasts
- ❖ Increased symptoms of estrogen deficiency
- ❖ Gastrointestinal bloating
- ❖ Candida exacerbation
- ❖ Drowsiness and excess sleep
- ❖ Mild depression

Total Estrogen - Having made it abundantly clear that there is no single estrogen, it would be prudent to test for the three "main" estrogens together.

- ❖ Determine the female appearance
- ❖ Allow ovulation to occur
- ❖ Important in lubrication of the mucous membrane (around the eyes, mouth, and vagina)
- ❖ Stimulates the central nervous system
- ❖ Improves the quality of skin, bones, and muscle
- ❖ Improves brain function
- ❖ Retains water and salt
- ❖ Relieves menopausal symptoms
- ❖ Increases female life expectancy
- ❖ Shields against coronary artery disease
- ❖ Helps prevent osteoporosis
- ❖ Protects against Alzheimer's disease

Symptoms of Low Estrogens

- ❖ Droopy, reduced, or overly small breasts
- ❖ Dry mucous membranes
- ❖ Short menses or long menstrual cycle
- ❖ Inadequate or lack of menses
- ❖ Headaches and migraines during menstruation
- ❖ Hair loss
- ❖ Fatigue
- ❖ Poor sex drive
- ❖ Cardiovascular disease
- ❖ Osteoporosis

Symptoms of Estrogens Deficiency

❖ Hot flashes
❖ Loss of libido
❖ Painful intercourse
❖ Vaginal dryness/atrophy
❖ Yeast infections
❖ Anxiety
❖ Depression
❖ Loss of memory
❖ Foggy thinking
❖ Dry skin
❖ Headaches and migraines
❖ Insomnia
❖ Heart palpitations
❖ Muscle and joint pain
❖ Bone loss
❖ Low mood and energy

Symptoms of Estrogens Dominance and Excess

❖ Menstrual cramps
❖ Heavy and irregular menses
❖ Breast swelling and tenderness
❖ Loss of sex drive
❖ Fluid retention
❖ Migraines
❖ Bloating
❖ Depression
❖ Mood swings
❖ Nervousness, anxiety, and irritability
❖ Weight gain
❖ Fatigue

❖ Craving for sweets
❖ Hair loss
❖ Symptoms of low thyroid
❖ Mental fuzz
❖ Fibrocystic breasts
❖ Uterine fibroids
❖ Endometriosis
❖ Hormone dependent cancers

As a clarification, we should mention that the difference between low and deficiency is a matter associated with age. Deficiency is the description of levels in old age when there is a chronic namesake deficiency of hormones.

Cortisol - The namesake hormone test.

Symptoms of High Cortisol

❖ Impaired mental performance
❖ Suppressed thyroid function
❖ Imbalances of glucose
❖ Decreased bone density
❖ Decreased muscle tissue
❖ Increased blood pressure
❖ Increased abdominal fat
❖ Depression
❖ Sleep Disturbances
❖ Low libido
❖ Anxiety
❖ Hair loss
❖ Elevated triglycerides

Symptoms of Low Cortisol

❖ Antisocial and criminal behavior
❖ Insomnia via adrenaline overload
❖ Heart palpitations
❖ Acne
❖ Fatigue
❖ Depression and panic attacks
❖ Irritability
❖ Infertility (via low progesterone)
❖ Migraine and headaches
❖ Fibromyalgia
❖ Cravings for sweets
❖ Allergies
❖ Chemical sensitivities
❖ Symptoms of low progesterone
❖ Symptoms of low thyroid hormone

TSH (Thyroid Stimulating Hormone) - Upon first glance one might assume that this is a thyroid hormone but not quite. Note that it's the hormone that stimulates the thyroid, and it is produced by the pituitary gland. Basically, this hormone tells the thyroid to create thyroid hormones when levels of said hormones are low. If the levels are high, production of TSH decreases. In short, the production of TSH helps keep the thyroid hormones in balance. For the purpose of restorative medicine optimized thyroid function is very important because it regulates how sensitive the body is to hormones in general.

Total Triiodothyronine (T3) - The more active thyroid hormone. Has extremely important functions such as the regulation of growth and development, heart rate, as well as assistance of metabolic and body temperature control. It has an effect on almost every physiological process in the body.

Total Thyroxine (T4) - Also plays a very important role in body metabolism, stimulating the consumption of oxygen in the body. T4 also converts into T3.

Thyroid Hormones

- ❖ Control cell growth and metabolism
- ❖ Help with weight management
- ❖ Improve heart and vascular health
- ❖ Renew energy
- ❖ Aid concentration
- ❖ Regulate body temperature

Symptoms of Low Thyroid Function

- ❖ Fatigue
- ❖ Cold extremities
- ❖ Low libido
- ❖ Dry skin
- ❖ General aches and pains
- ❖ Depression
- ❖ Scalp hair loss
- ❖ Brittle nails
- ❖ Low pulse and blood pressure
- ❖ Memory lapses
- ❖ Heart palpitations
- ❖ Constipation
- ❖ Low stamina
- ❖ Low body temperature
- ❖ Headaches
- ❖ Intolerance to cold

- ❖ Weight gain
- ❖ Anxiety
- ❖ Swollen, puffy eyes
- ❖ Poor concentration
- ❖ High cholesterol
- ❖ Infertility
- ❖ Fibromyalgia

C-Reactive Protein - Quite simply, this is a protein the level of which increases when there is inflammation in the body. As such, it can be an indicator for a variety of ailments ranging from arthritis and cancer to heart disease.

Prolactin - Perhaps the most known function of prolactin is in the link it has to lactation. Increasing levels of prolactin stimulate lactation post pregnancy once progesterone levels have decreased. Outside of such scenarios high levels of prolactin can point to issues such as sexual disorders or lack of menstruation.

Serotonin - This is a very important neurotransmitter associated with feelings of well-being and happiness, as well as a host of other functions. Many classes of drugs such as antidepressants and antipsychotics that alter serotonin levels. This also includes some of the most popular drugs dealing with anxiety as well.

25-Hydroxy Vitamin D - Though vitamin D is not technically a vitamin, it is nonetheless important in the human body. Mammals (and thus humans) synthesize vitamin D when sunlight hits the skin, as well as being able to acquire it through dietary means. It can also have an influence on cholesterol production.

Prostate Specific Antigen (PSA) - This male only test is for the measurement of PSA in the blood, elevated levels of which can potentially point to prostate cancer or an enlarged prostate.

Insulin-like Growth Factor (IGF-1) - This important protein has many functions, among them the regulation of growth of nearly every cell in the body. Low levels of this protein can point to issues such as cardiovascular disease.

Homocysteine - This is an amino acid high levels of which can point to an increased risk of cardiovascular disease.

Aldosterone - This test is not always performed but the function of aldosterone cannot be denied. It is actually the most potent hormone in the body in regards to the balance of electrolytes. It has regulatory effects on the metabolism of carbohydrates, regulates blood pressure, and can be employed for low blood pressure, hearing loss, tinnitus, and migraine.

Factory Grade Hormones and Horse Urine

With the blood tests covered you might go the second question posed regarding the safety of taking hormones. The ones in your body are certainly on the straight and narrow, but what about the ones you actually take? Certainly many have been showered with stories about hormones, side effects, and other just all around bad things with hormones.

This can be looked at from several directions. The first one is the word steroid, such as the full name of the *steroid* hormones that we have liberally been dropping all over the place. Steroid hormones are the ones produced in your body. Your body manufactures them, it uses them, and they are meant to be part of the overall human anatomical "ecosystem." However, that's definitely not the first association that pops into the minds of most people. The first thought that usually pops into the brain when the word steroid is heard is "those other" steroids. Well actually there is no "those other," because those steroids are synthetic anabolic steroids.

Synthetic anabolic steroids are drugs, key word being of course drugs, that are meant to imitate the effects of testosterone and dihydrotestosterone. Let's consider an ex United States president, and a person who looks a lot like this president and can talk like him. One of these individuals will provide a budget surplus, while the other one is going to look and sound a lot like the president. Which one would you prefer running your country? This is the problem with synthetic anabolic steroids and indeed any drugs that try to "mimic" what we have in our body.

These synthetic substances do not have the same chemical formulas as the ones inside of our body, because of course you can't patent the formula of the things in your body because that wouldn't make sense and you couldn't charge the proverbial arm and leg for it either. One could of course always think, what's the problem with maybe a little extra carbon here, maybe a bit of oxygen over there, in the chemical formula? The thing is, your body creates the chemical formulas it does for a reason - they work and are specifically made to carry out their proper functions. Synthetic imitators are recognized as the dirty infiltrators that they are and are not fully accepted by the body as a true replacement.

Let's use a commonly known example such as progestin, a synthetic progesterone used in large part for various birth control pills. In one study, women who used estrogen and progestin had a significantly higher risk of acquiring breast cancer, but women who used progesterone that was bio-identical, or identical to the one found in the body, had a decreased risk of breast cancer.[1] Another study that tried a combination of non-bioidentical estrogens and progestin had to be stopped before running it's course because risks for both heart attacks and breast cancer increased.[2]

There is another distinction that has to be made in regards to our usage of the term bio-identical hormone. When we refer to the use of bioidentical hormone supplementation, we are referring to bioidentical for the human body. Premarin, a popular estrogen replacement that has fallen out of use lately because of published studies regarding risks such as endometrial cancer,[3] is what you could technically call bioidentical. However, it is bioidentical in the sense that it comes from horses. To be more exact, estrogens derived from the urine of pregnant horses,

with part horse estrogen. Hence, the name - **PRE**gnant **MAR**es' ur**IN**e (someone get in touch with Interpol, we cracked the code). Now, we can't go around claiming to be all knowing experts about everything, but "word on the street" is that the human body is not exactly lacking in its production capacity of estrogen derived from the urine of horses who maybe had too much to drink one night and didn't use protection.

And that's the problem. Popular perception and mental imprinting associates the word steroids and hormones not with the natural ones made in the body, but those synthetic ones which from a chemical and biological standpoint do not belong in the body at all. When our ears hear estrogen, our brain pulls up all the bad things associated with pregnant mare urine extract (doesn't quite have the same ring as vanilla extract) and not the estrogens in our body. Reports and articles certainly don't help either, with many occasions where the word "estrogen" is used freely when the subject matter is about synthetic and not bioidentical hormones. But hey, who needs journalistic integrity and editorial fact checking when buzzwords and sensationalism sell articles?

Sealing the Compartments of a Sinking Ship

So the individualized approach covers both the hormones and the tests and creates a program for all the factors. How does the spread go? The most important thing to remember is the one to one approach. Pregnenolone for pregnenolone, DHEA for DHEA, so on and so forth, and not any kinds of mixture such as say combined pregnenolone and DHEA. Everything from the hormonal side is approached via the oral route other than the progesterone, estrogens, and the testosterone.

Now, ordinarily the oral route can be seen as a rather inflexible approach, and we would agree in the case of the last three hormones we just mentioned. However, in the case of something such as pregnenolone, an oral route can still be made easily modifiable. For example, let's say that based on the history and blood test, it is suggested that 75 mg of pregnenolone be used. The suggestion for a bottle of just 75 mg pregnenolone would not be given. Instead, the power of mathematics is brought in for consultation and something like 50 mg and 25 mg are suggested, which can be taken together and increased or decreased as needed. This is the approach taken with hormones of the oral sort.

The progesterone, estrogens, and testosterone are different. The use of an oral route is not followed because it is too inflexible. Instead, the gel-in-syringes approach is used. Just to be perfectly clear, that is the syringe with gel that is squeezed out and rubbed onto the skin, not a syringe with needle where gel is injected into the body, because that would probably be the definition of a bad time. This approach allows for the quick modulation of these hormones as well, because a compounded pill approach is very rigid and does not allow for the mirroring of the body's fluidity. In particular, this applies to progesterone and estrogens.

Part of the optimal female physiology during the early age is the cyclic nature of the menstrual period, which as we mentioned is caused by the fluctuation of progesterone and estrogens. The restorative approach takes this well into account and follows variable doses for the pattern of the menstrual cycle or via an artificial cycle for women post menopause. On top of the 1:1 hormone approach, there are other components of the program that are commonly used.

Melatonin, Morpheus' Confederate

Melatonin is a hormone, a neurohormone but not a steroid hormone, hence its omission from the main bunch before. The function that melatonin is perhaps best known for is its function within the circadian rhythm. The circadian rhythm is certainly not a human only phenomenon, and can be found in animals,

plants, and even bacteria. Basically, this rhythm is the description of biological function that differentiates based around the time of the standard Earth day of 24 hours via reactions from the surrounding environment by factors such as daylight.

Melatonin is also known as a "night" or "darkness" hormone because it is created when such conditions occur. The site of production of melatonin in the human body is the pineal gland mentioned before. It is an endocrine hormone and enters directly into the blood stream. When light enters the human eye, production of melatonin is suppressed. We can't simply refer to melatonin as the "go to sleep" hormone, of course, because if it's one thing we've learned so far is that hormonal labels are bad and every single hormone seems to be an over-achiever and wants to do many different jobs. Melatonin is also a potent antioxidant (we will cover these beneficial agents at a later point). Melatonin also plays a role in the cell death of cancers.[4] We will just end on melatonin being particularly good at its well-known job as a weapon in the battle against insomnia.

Magnesium, Brunch of Cellular Champions

While many people subconsciously accept the fact that the human body has some elements which might not sound like they belong there, such as iron in hemoglobin, there is perhaps not as much recognition of the importance of metals and their function in allowing us to live. Without the mentioned iron in our bloodstream, our body would not receive oxygen and oxygen is most definitely something that organisms at this point in Earth's time period like to use. We accept that iron supplements help with iron deficient anemia, but all the links on the cellular biological side are often not fully considered. Such is the case of magnesium.

When most people think of magnesium as it applies to the human body, they are likely to think of milk of magnesia, the common name of magnesium hydroxide. Magnesium hydroxide has two general uses: as an antacid and as a laxative, the latter being the more well-known use. Suffice to say, if a person is feeling "stopped up," a swig of the old milk of magnesia is liable to clear up even the most egregious of obstructions. But is that it? Is the sole role of magnesium to be a savior after a particularly over-indulgent night at an all you can eat Brazilian steakhouse?

Enter adenosine triphosphate (ATP). We won't linger on ATP too long because the most important thing to know about ATP is that we can think of it as the energy unit of cellular metabolism, and it is often called the energy currency of life because every cell has it and needs it. Mini high school biology refresher aside, what does this have to with magnesium? In order for mitochondria, the energy producing organelles within cells, to function and produce more ATP, it first needs to be powered by ATP that is bound to magnesium. How about that, magnesium? You just shot up from constipation aide to being absolutely vital for human survival. Knowing this vital function of magnesium leads to no surprise at the variability and potential severity of symptoms; starting on the mild level with muscle cramps and fatigue, moving up to full on muscle spasms and nausea, all the way up to heart failure.[5-7]

Magnesium can have a calming effect on the nervous system and as such can be a great aid in helping with issues ranging from headaches and migraine to muscle spasms. And yes, constipation, but magnesium doesn't appreciate being known only for that. Based on the symptoms and issues often presented in individuals who want to take the restorative medicine approach, magnesium is often a given recommendation. According to the Agricultural Research Service, which is part of the United States Department of Agriculture (USDA), 43% of the population in the United States receives adequate magnesium through diet, meaning of course that more than half don't.[8] We can safely say that the level of magnesium consumption in the United States is not "USDA choice."

Serotonin, Herald of Happiness

We already mentioned some of the benefits of serotonin, but wanted to stress that a different route must be taken when we're speaking about oral administration. Without going into too much detail, the blood brain barrier is the term for the separation of the blood circulating in our bodies from the fluid surrounding our brain, for everything to not go all over the place willy nilly. Basically, this is both a safeguard against foreign invaders such as bacteria but also so that the only things getting in, such as oxygen molecules or hormones, are the things that are needed in the brain in the first place.

Serotonin that is taken orally is not able to cross this barrier, and seeing as the effects of serotonin as a neurotransmitter can certainly be useful in our mental overseer composed entirely of neurons, this would be a problem. However, 5-Hydroxytryptophan (5-HTP) is a precursor of serotonin and melatonin that can in fact cross this blood brain barrier. This is why if an individual has inadequate the recommendation is not a "serotonin" supplement, but instead 5-HTP. You can eat avocados all day long, with their high serotonin content, but if it isn't getting through to the brain then all that guacamole was eaten for naught, though the tortilla chip manufacturing industry does thank you. The majority of serotonin is actually found in your intestines, though its effects on the brain cannot be understated. While serotonin binds to neurons and neurons can obviously be found throughout the body, the brain is a particularly important concentration of said neurons with many specific functions other than "ouch fire hot".

Intestinal Flora, the Great Absorbers

This term is code for the restoration of the good bacteria that live in your intestines at this very moment, because they're in there, moving around, and helping you stay healthy (we apologize for the mental image of trillions of living organisms moving around in your bowels). While the term bacteria usually brings to mind those disease causing blighters, there are a lot of good bacteria, especially in our gastrointestinal system. This restoration or optimization is accomplished by the taking of what is called probiotics, a term certainly familiar to many people via yogurt commercials because if those commercials are to be believed then when commercial actors aren't acting, they're chronically constipated and need probiotics to stay regular.

The well-known role of intestinal flora is in it's function of digestion and absorption. While the stomach and intestines already do a bang up job in this department, the bacteria living in those parts help speed things along or even to help us break down what we normally couldn't. A good example for this is termites. They don't just eat wood and digest it themselves - the relationship that they have with the organisms in their gut allows them to digest the cellulose from the wood. In fact, the protozoa living there help with this function, and those protozoa themselves have symbiotic bacteria that help them in this function. It seems that termites have many more beneficial symbiotic associations than we give them credit for, but not when those little devils are eating our brand new timber cottage. The bacteria in our human digestive system go after some carbohydrates, such as certain starches and fibers, because we lack certain enzymes for their digestion. Ultimately, through their actions bacteria provide the human body with energy and nutrients that we would otherwise miss out on.

Good digestion and absorption are not the only aspects that intestinal flora help us with. They are also responsible for boosting our overall immune system by helping prevent the growth of pathogenic bacteria, the kind we certainly don't want, in our digestive tract. This hefty "us or them" approach allows beneficial bacteria to flourish and bring in more of their type while trying to keep the bad ones out in the rain. Intestinal flora can also potentially help with allergy prevention and inflammatory bowel disease such as Crohn's. Serotonin is also produced in the intestines.

One must always keep in mind that when bad bacteria set up shop in our body, we are often prescribed antibiotics. Unfortunately, while the bacteria in our intestines have friend or foe targeting, the antibiotic won't hear any of that. When the antibiotic goes to work, it gets down to business and likes to annihilate everything in its path. While that tends to kill our foreign invaders, it also causes some serious Dresden bombing action on our civilian bacteria population. Hence, the reason that antibiotics have the common side effect of diarrhea is because your native population of the Home Team is suddenly at a disadvantage.

Saw Palmetto, Blocker of Receding Hairlines

When we say saw palmetto, we aren't referring to the leaves or some kind of ground up paste from saw palmetto, which is a type of palm. What we refer to is more specifically the extract from the fruit of the saw palmetto. The reason for this is because it functions as an inhibitor of the actions of 5-alpha reductase. We generally try to stay away from enzyme names because the learned men behind their naming tried their utmost to keep them out of ordinary conversation with all their hyphens and most unnatural composition.

Back to the matter at hand, 5-alpha reductase is the enzyme that you would have seen in our chart as being the intermediary between testosterone and dihydrotestosterone (DHT). So why in the world would we want to tell 5-alpha to hold its reins here and there? To answer that question, we have to look at DHT.

DHT is extremely potent. If testosterone is the most cut and muscular guy at the gym benching 150 kilograms, DHT is the bigger guy having a bit of a laugh as he prepares to do his set of 400 kilograms with no spotter (because he doesn't need one and will get angry if you suggest otherwise). Basically, anywhere testosterone can perform, DHT can outperform. It is much more prone to attachment to testosterone receptors and is just more potent overall, with about 5% of testosterone going over to become DHT. One might think, what's the big deal? If there is this super testosterone floating about, why would we not like that?

Being bald comes to mind with DHT being the main culprit behind male pattern baldness, and to a lesser extent the female variety (more factors go into female hair loss). It is also a contributor to benign prostate hyperplasia (BPH) due to its effect on prostate enlargement.[9] BPH is simply code for enlargement of the prostate gland without that nasty association of prostate cancer. While there are certain parts of the "groin region" that some men would wish to be enlarged, having a prostate swelling to grapefruit proportions is not what they have in mind.

DHT laughs at men in more ways, though not fully by its fault. Consider the big picture, as we are always trying to do when speaking about how complex our body system is. You saw the side effects that can come with the age related decline of hormone production, so let's put some factors together. A man in the prime of his life starts to age in the bad direction, because that harlot mother nature is out to get him. All those hormones begin to decline, and then the body thinks, oh man, you guys have to listen to this because I have a great idea. Testosterone is falling, but we got that old boy DHT to save the day. He's way more potent than testosterone, which we don't have enough of anymore to be all man. What's a logical step to take?

Try to produce more DHT through conversion of course. On paper, it makes sense because DHT is stronger and thus should technically pick up the slack by the lowered testosterone level. However, taking into consideration all the factors at play here including slowly elevating estrogen levels in men as they age, this is not the best of ideas the body has had. In short, the correction of applying more potency backfires. What we wind up is not a favored bald movie star, as the body would believe it is making. No, what we wind up with is Uncle Mark in his grape jelly stained tank top, sweat pants, and sandals who is afflicted by male pattern baldness, a pot belly, love handles gymnasts could hang on to for complex maneuvers, and a prostate that sends him to the urinal every 10 minutes during your annual trip to Disney World.

Zinc, Catalyst and Man Keeper

Zinc plays many important roles in the body. These various performances include such things as ensuring prostate gland function,[10] functioning as a widespread catalyst for many enzyme reactions, and even in the metabolism of RNA and DNA, the keepers of our genetic information. It has even been shown to be part of an efficient treatment approach in age related macular degeneration. We will cover macular degeneration in slightly more detail down the line, but for now can simply refer to it as a condition of retinal damage that slowly causes the afflicted to lose full use of their sight, sometimes even resulting in blindness.[11] Suffice to say, the importance of zinc in processes of biological nature cannot be overstated.

For our purposes here, we simply want to mention why the use of zinc is employed in the hormonal restorative approach. If you go back up to our chart, you can put in the enzyme aromatase between testosterone and estradiol. As men age, this process can tend to increase. While we made it abundantly clear that estrogens play important roles in men, too many estrogens are not the best thing for men because such is the domain of women and symptoms of excess estrogens can hit men just as hard (say hello to your new friends the love handles). Zinc factors into this because it works as an aromatase inhibitor.

This works on several levels in the approach. Older men who are having issues with elevated estrogens due to an excess of this conversion can benefit via lower levels of estrogens. Even obesity can make the process of aromatization kick into higher gear. Individuals using testosterone supplementation can benefit as well to prevent any extra conversion from going on.

As We Stand Here Amongst All These Old Trees

As you read all the information presented so far, you might think - but no, my hormones are fine. I had a blood test recently and I actually checked some of these things out and it said that I was fine and within my range for everything. This is what we have to look at next to fully clarify this situation of ranges.

The most important thing to remember is that when the reference range is mentioned, statistics rears its big giant ugly head and starts grouping people. This is very nice, because we need to have distinctions and subsets of populations so that we can accurately study what all is going on. However, in this case, this doesn't help us that much when we consider where we want to be at as opposed to where we are now.

Let's say that you are in your 70's and aren't as spry as a young elm tree anymore, and your daughter and her family are over to visit. This includes your favorite grandchildren. But mercy me, those grandchildren just won't shut up and stop running around. They keep asking you to play tag with them but the jig is up because they have the advantage. Maybe your daughter told them about the will that leaves them with the catfish farm and they want to expedite that process by giving you a heart attack. How else are they going to pay for college to get a degree so that they can't get a job due to an unemployable major?

You feel old. You got plenty of friends your age at your local backgammon club, and they all feel old too. Some of them whisper fearfully that their grandchildren are out to get them as well. These compatriots of your age and you yourself are feeling over the hill, you are seemingly past your prime, and you don't feel too hot because of that. But you can see it now in your head, as clear as a dehydrated alcoholic stranded in the Sahara sees a rum factory glimmering above the dunes, that all those test results are in "your range." But who is in your range?

Everyone at your backgammon club. Everyone who "feels their age" and feels just as old and worn out as you. This is your reference range. Now look back to your 20s, when you felt great, when birds were singing in the air and the threat of communism loomed like a rapidly deflating hot air balloon. If you had checked your blood tests at that time (and were also a time traveler because some such tests did not exist back then), then you would have likely been in your "reference range" as well.

At both times you would be in your reference range. The main difference is that at one end of that time, you are in the reference range during the prime of your life, while on the other end you are the reference range of "maybe I should go visit Paris because I can't remember where I buried my chest of gold anymore and that dumb farmer in a black robe keeps following me around and waving at me." Now consider how you would like to feel - old and worn out, or young and vigorous (that might be rhetorical)? To achieve some manner of restoration towards that energy and function, you would have to place yourself in the reference range of yourself in the 20s and away from your backgammon club range.

This is the way that the restorative approach seeks to further its goals. What is the point of being at a good level in your reference range when that range is meant to confine you to the levels where so much of your good functions from the Jazz Age are impaired? The approach seeks to restore your levels to those of a healthy person of your gender who is 20-29 years old. As we mentioned earlier, this is that golden time period when you can go trapping beavers on the frontier because you still feel great, that time before all those pesky associations with low hormone levels begin to crop up due to your advancing age. What follows is the range then, the optimal one, and not the backgammon one.

Steroid Hormone Range for Women	Reference Range (20-29 year old bracket)	The Optimal Range
Pregnenolone	10-230 ng/dL	157-230 ng/dL
Total Estrogen	61-437 pg/mL	150-437 pg/mL*
Progesterone	0.2-28 ng/mL	1-28 ng/mL*
DHEA-Sulfate	65-380 ug/dL	275-380 ug/dL
Total Testosterone	14-76 ng/dL	55-76 ng/dL
Cortisol (tested in the AM)	4.3-22.4 ug/dL	16.4-22.4 ug/dL

*(depends on the phase of the menstrual cycle)

Steroid Hormone Range for Men	Reference Range (20-29 year old bracket)	The Optimal Range
Pregnenolone	10-200 ng/dL	137-200 ng/dL
Total Testosterone	241-827 ng/dL	632-827 ng/dL
DHEA-Sulfate	280-640 ug/dL	520-640 ug/dL
Total Estrogen	0-130 pg/mL	<43 pg/mL
Progesterone	0.3-1.2 ng/mL	0.9-1.2 ng/mL
Cortisol (tested in the AM)	4.3-22.4 ug/dL	16.4-22.4 ug/dL

As seen in these charts, we have the reference range of the decade of life that we want to try and rekindle, as well as the optimal range. It stands to reason that based on the information available, with issues associated with lower levels and benefits associated with higher levels, that simply being in the reference range is not fully indicative of the greatest benefit that can be received. After all, a pregnenolone level of 15 is within the reference range, but isn't exactly what one would want when trying to fight off possibly encroaching dementia. The only thing worse than having spiders in your room at night, is forgetting if you have spiders in your room at night. The optimal range is then the roughly upper one third of the reference range here. So, let's sum up how this all works.

- ❖ History of symptoms and issues is provided and read, blood tests are looked at.
- ❖ A program made to cover the issues is created while following several core tenants: convenience in regards to taking only what is needed the most and affordability, specific application against issues and values, wholly

individualized for each person, and extreme modularity in program design for quick modification potential.

❖ The assessment of feedback from the user delivered as frequently as needed for possible program modification.

❖ Regular blood tests at varying intervals (3-6 months) for further adjustments and assessment

This is the summarized approach. In an earlier part, we already mentioned the issues associated with low levels of various hormones. We have also described symptoms of deficiency, imbalance, or excess when it comes to steroid hormones. We will also be going into various other deficiencies and disease that can have an application in the restorative medicine approach.

At this point you might be thinking something, something important. We spoke at length about certain issues, but you may have noticed that something was lacking from the discussion, something that is on the mind of millions concerned with their health. Cholesterol was referenced earlier, but it seems like mum's the word now, with nary a mention. This is because cholesterol is one to watch out, a very important topic to discuss and we thought it important to devote some time speaking about it. So let's take a look and see what cholesterol's deal is, and why it seems to act like such a big jerk.

Cholesterol and Prometheus have some things in common. They achieved bad boy status while doing something good and then got hung in the court of public opinion.

PART V

On the Nature of Cholesterol

High cholesterol. The very phrase probably sends shivers up the spines of many, bringing about thoughts of something bad in our body slowly digging away our grave at the local cemetery. Everywhere we turn, the eternal war against cholesterol rages on (and by eternal we mean starting late in the previous 20th century). We certainly have a lot of help from many sources who we can thank. A brief stroll through the grocery store shows those convenient butter like substances that have low cholesterol, and even certain breakfast cereals have cholesterol lowering properties. The friendly ~~paid actors~~ doctors and patients on all those television commercials seek to educate us by repeating that high cholesterol just might be responsible for buying us a first class ticket across the Styx. Why, even those nice people at the pharmaceutical companies are helping us out with lower prices on generic cholesterol lowering drugs because their patent expired.

Well, it is very reassuring to all of us that so many people and companies care about our high cholesterol! However, some, or even many of us, may have questions. Rampant consumerism is certainly a wonderful teacher, because if so many people spend so much money working and advertising a way down from the Cholesterol Mountains, why then certainly it must be a good idea. But then, regardless of the popular opinion, some people might want to throw caution into the wind and learn something for themselves. So what about this cholesterol then?

Let's approach it from the most popular direction. Is it something that we eat in our daily food, the overindulgence of which can lead to greatly increased levels? Cholesterol levels are usually mentioned in tandem with triglycerides, after all, and triglycerides compromise a large part of fat in humans. Not to mention that all those cholesterol lowering commercials are always talking about "along with diet and exercise." Cholesterol can indeed be what is termed "dietary cholesterol," or simply put cholesterol that we gain from food. However, dietary cholesterol as a whole makes up a small amount of our cholesterol. So where, then does the impish spawn come from?

Turns out from our own bodies. Great, so not only is mother nature out to get us in general with that whole "age thing" while cars and television sets can increase our risk of heart disease, but now our OWN body is in on the whole scheme as well. Ok, maybe the body is having a bad time or is under duress to create what seems like such a dangerous compound. Let's take a look at where this vile substance is in our bodies.

We can take a look at the liver. Why the liver? Because the liver is actually a production site of both triglycerides and cholesterol. Well that's nice, not only is the liver always on our case about keeping it "healthy" and not to overindulge in the partaking of half a liter of fruity alcoholic drinks, but now it has the audacity to manufacture that garbage in our body? The betrayal doesn't end there. The liver twists the proverbial dagger in our backs by not only creating cholesterol, but also by sending it out all throughout our bodies. It even takes some of it back in, reabsorbing it to create more of the vile stuff. Whatever, liver.

You think you got the upper hand now, but we're going with this information to head honcho. That's right, the jig is up because we are going to tell the brain all about your little plan here to kill off the body!

So let's tell the brain. Hold on now, something seems off. The brain, it is tainted with cholesterol as well. Heavens to Betsy, what in the name of Nikola Tesla's alternating current is going on here? Seems like the brain is not only held under gunpoint by cholesterol, it is actually another site of production. Because of the blood brain barrier that we mentioned earlier, cholesterol cannot get through to the brain from the blood. Therefore, any cholesterol around the brain, which accounts for a decent bit of cholesterol in general, is produced on site. To top it all off, cholesterol is embedded in myelin, a substance which forms a protective sheath around axons, which are the parts of neurons that send messages to other neurons.

Are we all lost? Is every human being on the planet aboard the RMS Cholesterol Titanic headed for the iceberg? Not only is cholesterol around the areas where our nerves are sending information, it is also present in cell membranes, which are some would say a necessary part of the cell. We just can't seem to get away from it.

This is all starting to sound like the bad plot of some made for TV movie with an antagonist who knows no equal and cannot be stopped. A logical individual would answer, but that's not exactly the point, is it? The thing that everyone is looking at is the different types of cholesterol right? There is always mention about keeping your good cholesterol up and your bad cholesterol down. Let's take a look at cholesterol itself and see if we can get to the bottom of all this from the chemical approach.

Cholesterol, Defiler of Logic

What is cholesterol? Cholesterol is cholesterol. If that sounds maddeningly simplistic and unexplainable, that's because it is. While it is referred to as frequently as a lipid, fat, or steroid, cholesterol doesn't appreciate that because it doesn't quite fit any of those descriptions one to one. Sometimes it is even called a combination of a steroid and alcohol, but it doesn't behave like an alcohol. It seems like cholesterol is always trying to be the rebel. Or perhaps it is that proverbial bad cholesterol that is the rebel, while good cholesterol is trying to fight the good fight?

This is where we run into a problem of classification. Perhaps it is not so much a problem, as much as a blatant incorrect label. Basically, bad cholesterol is the term for low density lipoproteins (LDL), while good cholesterol is the term for high density lipoproteins (HDL). You might ask, but why isn't the actual word cholesterol in those titles? It isn't because they aren't cholesterol. They belong to the group of players who are known as variable transports for triglycerides, phospholipids, cholesterol, cholesteryl esters, and proteins. Going in order from largest to smallest, they are chylomicrons, very low density lipoproteins (VLDL), intermediate density lipoproteins (IDL), LDL, and HDL.

While we can provide brief summaries of action, we don't want to go too much into details and variable percentages of composition to bog down the flow. Chylomicrons are responsible for getting the cholesterol and "fats" from our diet from the intestines and bringing it to the liver for assimilation and future use. VLDL is the next transport and unlike chylomicrons, VLDL transport products actually made inside the body, as opposed to those taken in by the actions of the chylomicrons. IDL are more temporary in nature and simply ferry items back to the liver.

LDL, or "bad cholesterol," is a transport of both cholesterol created within the body due to local synthesis as well as cholesterol taken in externally through diet. It is also the primary transport of cholesterol and accounts for more than 50% of all circulating lipids, bringing cholesterol to where it is needed. LDL is involved in the formation of those atherosclerotic plaques on artery walls that we talked about earlier. Meanwhile, HDL works like a vacuum cleaner, sucking up any cholesterol that wasn't used by cells and bring it back to the liver. From there, the cholesterol is either re-assimilated to be used later or given the boot via bile. For individuals wanting a little bit of hard numbers for composition, here is a reference chart for the actual numbers. Before you inquire on the chart, an ester is a chemical compound derived from something.

	Triglycerides	Cholesterol Esters	Cholesterol	Phospholipids	Proteins
Chylomicrons	85-88%	3%	1%	8%	1-2%
VLDL	50-55%	12-15%	8-10%	18-20%	5-12%
IDL	24-30%	32-35%	8-10%	25-27%	10-12%
LDL	10-15%	37-48%	8-10%	20-28%	20-22%
HDL	3-15%	15-30%	2-10%	24-46%	55%

Something from this table[1] might have caught your eye. This something might have been the fact that not a single one of those transporters comes even close to a 100% value of cholesterol. Why is that relevant to our discussion? We are talking about "bad cholesterol" and "good cholesterol." Such a name implies cholesterol, with no ifs or buts about it. Based on those percentages listed, not a single one of those lipid transports can be simply called or even close to being called "cholesterol," because it makes no sense. One might argue that based on what we saw of the jobs of LDL and HDL, that the bad and good labels are somewhat appropriate.

However, that has no bearing whatsoever on the fact that the word "cholesterol" is there with the only adjectives adjacent to it being good or bad. This gives people who trust the industry for reliable information an impression that there are two types of cholesterol, and one of those types of cholesterol is out to get them. This nomenclature, coupled with the huge push to just plain lower cholesterol values or keep them down, gives cholesterol overall a bad name. But of course there is only one type of cholesterol.

Before we go further, it might be prudent to note how the very popular lipid profile test is accomplished in the blood testing laboratory. On first glance, one might see that the value is right there in the test - total cholesterol, printed out clear as the Mississippi River. But then, right below that value you will notice three to four other names - HDL, LDL, Triglycerides, and sometimes VLDL. What impact do they have on the number of your total cholesterol? According to the formula, they are your total cholesterol.

$$\text{Total Cholesterol} = \text{HDL} + \text{LDL} + \frac{\text{Triglycerides}}{5}$$

One might be liable to say that based on our previous observation and analysis of composition, this might not be the most accurate display of "cholesterol." Can it give us an idea of how many transport molecules there are moving to and fro? Sure, but if cholesterol is popularly classified as a WMD, then it would be nice to see if the trucks transporting said weapons are empty, full, or maybe just one warhead shy of being half full.

HDL, LDL, and VLDL are added together to create your total cholesterol value. In times when triglycerides are tested, this value is divided by five to receive an estimation of the amount of VLDL. However, one might say triglycerides are not liable to be called cholesterol, because they aren't cholesterol at all. They are in fact an excellent method of storing excess calories that we consume that are not readily utilized. In essence, a food that is practically fat-free but has an immense carbohydrate content can increase the production of triglycerides if you eat it in excess, which has the potential for throwing off levels off without the direct involvement of cholesterol. The point of all this is that whether you are testing for the three lipoproteins or the two lipoproteins and triglycerides, you are not directly measuring the level of actual cholesterol. The label "total cholesterol" is inherently flawed because this is a test for the amount of carriers in the blood which all have variable amounts of actual cholesterol.

In our description of the actions of LDL and HDL, you might have noticed the use of concepts using cholesterol or bringing it to where it was needed. We already mentioned that cholesterol is in the cell membranes, so perhaps we should further that example. The cell membrane surrounds all cells, thus constituting a large part of what defines a cell. They play a large role in maintaining homeostatic balance, or equilibrium, in the cell compared to the outside environment as well as generally letting in what is needed while expelling what needs to be out or along on its way. The main point is that without a functional cell membrane, there is no cell to speak of. Cholesterol is a major building block of these cell membranes. At this point a person might, just might, say that cholesterol seems to be somewhat important in the body in certain regards.

Working Day and Night

Let's take a look at high and low cholesterol. The proper name for high cholesterol is hypercholesterolemia, the one which is also associated with atherosclerosis. However, we will simply refer to it as high cholesterol because the individuals behind the name hypercholesterolemia did not take into consideration the movements of the tongue in trying to say that name over and over again. As we briefly mentioned earlier and will go into more detail soon, atherosclerosis is the buildup of plaque on the arteries which contains cholesterol, among other things. Whenever high cholesterol is seen, the worry that atherosclerosis is lurking in the bushes is of great concern to all involved. But what exactly are some of the indicators or issues that we can associate with both high and low cholesterol?

Before we begin looking at all examples, let's start the game with a curveball. First, let's look at some instances where the presence of high cholesterol is in no way malefic. What is one of the things that is most not associated with illness and death? The creation of life, of course. In this case, we can talk about pregnancy because there is certainly nothing malefic about a pregnant woman (though husbands going on midnight runs for Mongolian beef might disagree). What does a pregnant woman have to do with elevated cholesterol? A lot, apparently. Total cholesterol, LDL, and triglycerides all increase significantly during pregnancy, up to the seemingly coronary narrowing amount of 314 mg/dL.[2-7]

Nobody can deny that the number we just wrote is high. But pregnancy is something as basic as human life itself, because that is how we keep increasing our numbers. Are pregnant women falling over left and right from high cholesterol? One would say no, though if a woman later in her pregnancy does fall over, she will certainly need help getting back up because it's harder to stand up what with a person growing inside you. The familiar and inappropriate term for women as "baby factories" is quite an apt description when speaking without the sexist overtone. What does a factory do? It puts together a bunch of smaller parts or ingredients to make a completed product, though in this case the finished product is not rolls of string cheese or a hybrid car, but rather an average nine pound baby that most mothers might say has a very rude, unorthodox, and painful way of entering the world.

After the child is delivered, the mother's levels of total cholesterol decreases in great measure in the three month post mark and then a further decrease in the next nine months.[8] One might presume that this increased level is going up due to all the construction going around in the uterus, since growing a new person requires a lot of new cell membranes to be formed. In fact, if cholesterol and LDL levels are overall diminished during a pregnancy, there is a bigger threat of miscarriage.[9] Ok, right now we are going to think outside the box, so work with us here. Let's say that there's something, anything at all will do in our case, that in the appropriate amounts will help a woman keep a pregnancy and in decreased amounts will increase her risk of a terminated pregnancy. Would you in any way of approaching this statement call that something "bad" or want to decrease the level of? Unless you are an individual bent on the extermination of mankind, the answer is probably "why in the world would we want to"? Just some food for thought.

Let's keep riding the creation train a while longer and look at children. High cholesterol was found in up to 53.1% of children of school going age.[10-14] What an outrage. Where are all the statin drug commercials for little Timmy? Certainly a lot of older people riding bikes in those advertisements, maybe Timmy wants to get in on the action too, but how can he with high cholesterol? Perhaps, in a glorious period of illumination, logic would dictate that in such cases these cholesterol levels are associated with construction and growth. Sabotaging that process via artificial lowering would probably not be the best idea.

Pregnant women and children aside, there are also examples of adults in the purely building up process. When athletes are training for sports such as hockey or soccer, their cholesterol levels show an increase.[15] Consider this example. People who play such sports professionally are trained to endure a lot of physical punishment. Soccer players have to keep up a quick pace for long stretches of time during a game and learn how the expertly fall down so as to give opposing players yellow cards, while hockey can be a pretty violent contact sport and there are no pirouettes on this ice - only blood. Anyone who says that individuals in such sports are not fit and healthy is either a fan of the other team or hasn't seen the amount of fake teeth in the hockey leagues.

Cholesterol's Bargain with the Reaper

Let's take a brisk but not pleasant walk through cholesterol and the associations that we have in regards to people dying, which is a very important association because death is something we want to stay far away from. Let's look at the straight association, the one that all these cholesterol lowering measures are trying to prevent - death related to heart disease. High cholesterol is most certainly a huge risk factor for atherosclerosis and myocardial infarction.[16,17] But then, the major issue is that when cholesterol levels are lowered through the popular method of cholesterol lowering drugs the overall rate of death is not offset by the number of people not dying due to heart attack.[18,19]

Let's consider both ends of the spectrum. Both high and low cholesterol are associated with an increased risk of premature death.[20] Does that do anything for us? We have to consider that extremes of any sort can be associated with negative things. Coffee that is too hot burns our tongue and prevents us from enjoying more of that sweet caffeine and coffee that is too cold can quickly turn into a popsicle, except boiling or frozen coffee doesn't increase your risk of dying. Though we wouldn't advise on driving down the highway with a topless coffee mug.

Let's take a look at hospitalized people for examples of how cholesterol works out in this regard. Now generally, people don't exactly want to pay the nightly cost of a hospital room so if an individual is healthy, he isn't going to be kicking it back and enjoying the fine selection of hospital pudding flavors. In one observation, the average cholesterol levels of hospitalized individuals who died as opposed to those who lived to fight another day were a good bit lower compared to the ones who kept fighting on.[21] In this case the difference in average levels is between 163.6 mg/dL and 217.8 mg/dL. Two things might jump out immediately from those numbers: the first is that the difference is actually pretty sizeable, and the second is that the latter number is above the normal range of 200 mg/dL. Another study of hospitalized individuals over the age of 65 showed that lower cholesterol levels were a predictor of an increased risk of death.[22] In this particular case the level range that was in most danger was below 160 mg/dL.

What about coronary heart disease itself? We know that there is a large association between cholesterol and atherosclerosis, what about people actually dying from this disease? People with cholesterol levels which were below 160 mg/dL actually had the highest rate of death in such cases while those with levels above 240 mg/dL had the lowest risk of death.[23] One would expect such a result to not occur at all. Meanwhile individuals older than 70 years with increased total cholesterol levels, low "good cholesterol," and high ratios of total cholesterol to HDL did not have overall increased death, increased death from coronary heart disease, or hospitalization resulting from heart attacks.[24] For men, the lowest amount of overall death was observed in the range between 180 and 239 mg/dL and decreasing it below this range resulted in increased risks from cancer and other diseases.[25]

These seem like big hits below the belt all around. First, high cholesterol doesn't appear to be nearly as big a scourge as it is made out to be, especially when speaking about the rates of death which should be the prime indicators about the overall danger of something. Second, low cholesterol actually appears to be worse off in allowing people to survive when they check in to a hospital and survival is oddly enough the primary reason that most people become hospitalized rather than letting things "run their course." Even the old "good cholesterol" doesn't seem to be as great as they say.

In fact, if HDL gets such a good rap, being good and all, then why aren't there drugs that simply raise HDL? Actually, this was in fact a considered option, but because of certain issues this drug never saw the light of day. What could possibly be an issue from a drug that raises good cholesterol, one might say? During human trials of the drug Torcetrapib, risk of death was increased by 59% and the risk of heart issues also increased by 25%. This seems really strange, because on the hypothetical paper where written out things make sense this would seem to, based on public perception that is, but in our case we would want a deeper look at it as always.

Let's think about HDL's function as we briefly looked at it. One of its jobs is to wander about the body to pick up and salvage cholesterol wherever it may be found so that it can be brought back to the liver for re-absorption. One interesting aspect of HDL is an almost chameleon like property, where in the standard phase it is anti-inflammatory, but during an acute phase response it becomes pro-inflammatory. This makes the seemingly "good" become a "bad," because it increases the risk of atherosclerosis.[26]

Let's look at it step by step with the inclusion of a drug that artificially increases HDL. In a well-balanced system, HDL is keeping the equilibrium up by taking the cholesterol that isn't used back so that it can be infused back into the system. Now let's introduce a gluttonous mass of HDL without the associated increase of cholesterol. Suddenly this pillaging horde is trying to take more cholesterol out of the system than should be taken out. If you keep picking the pepperoni off the pizza then you'll wind up with a cheese pizza, which might not be what you were in the market for. Except instead of having a subpar pizza, you are more likely to die or have issues with your heart.

Immune Support and Revelations

Let's get away from overall death as a statistical observation for a bit, important as it is when speaking about cholesterol, and look at something that might not be thought of as cholesterol's strong point, or any point at all for that matter. We might still be looking at death, but let's look at it from the viewpoint of immune system function and the relationship that might be present between it and cholesterol. Cancer is certainly something that we can associate with impaired immune function. If we aren't talking external factors like heavy doses of radiation, part of a cancer's possible progression is because the immune system suddenly finds that it didn't pick off that one straggler cell that won't know when to die properly and is now multiplying all over the place. The problem with this is that because we are not planted firmly in comic book lore, uncontrolled cell growth leads not to super regenerative abilities but to cancer that has the capacity to kill.

People suffering from advanced lung cancer, lymphoma, and cervical cancer had cholesterol levels that were lower in comparison to their healthy control group.[27] Low cholesterol in men was associated with higher incidences of colon and stomach cancers, as well as cancers in other locations.[28,29] There is even an inverse correlation between total cholesterol and LDL levels in association with incidence of cancer.[30,31] Suffice to say, that is an awful lot of cancer associated with lower cholesterol values.

Decreased cholesterol isn't only locked to cancer associations. There is also an association between decreased levels of cholesterol and increased rates of hospitalization from pneumonia and the flu for people in general as well as increased hospitalization from chronic obstructive pulmonary disease in men.[32] The flu is a bit heavier than the common cold, and people do die from it every year. However, all in all, for a healthy individual the potential yearly scuffle with influenza is usually a miserable affair but hardly hospital worthy. The fact that a decreased cholesterol value might be a deciding factor in having to drink some extra hot tea as opposed to spending time in the hospital just might be a cause for concern for some people. As for chronic obstructive pulmonary disease - if there is one thing more annoying than having lung function be obstructed, it is being hospitalized with obstructed lung function.

Decreased cholesterol levels seem to be associated with changes in how the body functions when it is undergoing an inflammatory response from infections.[33] As we mentioned before the actual inflammation process is your own body reacting to the invasion and being a little overzealous in the defense effort. Low cholesterol seems to be a marker for increased risk for HIV in men as well as being associated with immune system impairment while infected by this virus.[34,35] We can look at this just like the influenza hospitalization, where something already not great is made worse. In this particular case the link is perhaps even more significant because the way in which HIV works is by going to town on the immune system. Not to mention that HIV is quite a bit more severe than the seasonal flu. We can briefly observe hospitalized patients again and see that individuals who have low cholesterol prior to going under the knife for surgery have a greater occurrence of infections after the operation takes place.[36]

Oh Cholesterol, You Crafty Devil

All right, this is probably starting to make about as much sense as that time we got inebriated and tried to read *Crime and Punishment*. Cholesterol doesn't exactly seem to be out to get us on a widespread scale. Far from it, seems that it actually plays a role in building up our bodies as well as the creation and maturation of humans in general. It is certainly associated with total death, but almost certainly not in the way that we are used to hearing about it. On top of all that, it seems to be a very good predictor of helping us fight off cancers, infections, and disease. What in the Sam Hill is going on with this sorcery?

Now we introduce the full extent of cholesterol's power. Are we finally going to showcase the functions that make cholesterol to be the great antagonist that wants us dead? Will we finally see what crimes against humanity this molecule has concocted? Maybe not so much. We present to you, exhibit A.

The Sinister Role of Cholesterol

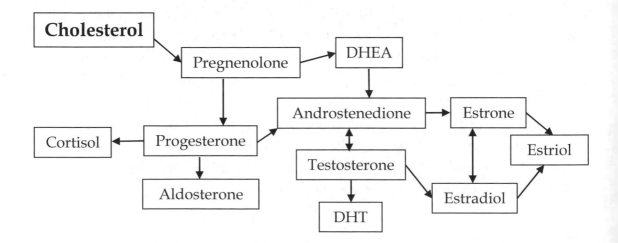

What manner of dark magic is this? What is cholesterol doing on that chart, the chart associated with steroid hormones and all the good things that they do? As it turns out, the steroid hormones are actually made from cholesterol. An enzyme hits cholesterol with several big smacks across the face and thus pregnenolone is created. What follows is that the origination of the steroid hormones comes from cholesterol.

Pregnenolone, which has vital functions and starts the conversion to all the other steroid hormones. DHEA, which is found throughout the body in large quantities. Testosterone, which makes men what they are and keeps the brain working properly. Estrogens which define women and provide a wealth of benefits in the body. Aldosteronealph, which helps regulate salt balance and has an impact on blood pressure. All these very important chemical messengers which help the human body to be created and function properly are created from public enemy numero uno.

We've said plenty about the merits of a restorative medicine approach, so what about this? How does the restorative approach work with high cholesterol, and why is there such a rampant distribution of high cholesterol all over the place? If we didn't have an answer to these questions, we probably wouldn't have written them out. Because that would be pretty embarrassing.

The "Cholesterol is a Pretty Cool Guy" Hypothesis

Granted, we don't call it that. If you approach problems scientifically, then you have to give them boring scientific names. Ok, here is the rub - our hypothesis is that steroidopenia is a result of aging and as such is a primary mechanism of hypercholesterolemia which then itself is identified as a consequence of age-related, enzyme-dependent down regulation of steroid hormone biosynthesis and their interconversions. Also known as the **hormonodeficit hypothesis of hypercholesterolemia** (hooray for alliteration). See what happened there? All the fun is just magically sucked out of the room. Just right out. Close the window, because there is a giant science tornado outside and all the fun is getting blown right out. Let's break that down for the benefit of what we're sure are the scant few among us who don't have an advanced in born comprehension of chemical and biological principles backed up by a rich knowledge of Latin.

We can knock off steroidopenia first, because that's a simple one. Penia is from the Latin for deficiency, and steroids we don't have to explain because surely you've been paying attention this whole time. Jam those two together and what we have is literally the deficiency of steroid hormones. Hypercholesterolemia we already explained to be the name for high cholesterol that we avoid saying because it isn't kind to the mouth. Enzyme dependent calls back to the little detail we mentioned about enzymes and how they are instrumental in the conversion processes between steroid hormones. Down regulation is simply a reference to the decrease of cellular components in response to an external variable. Biosynthesis is more evidence of Latin at work and refers to the conversion of products into more complex ones with the influence of enzymes.

Let's translate that into the common tongue of men then. Elevated levels of cholesterol can occur when steroid hormone levels are decreased, because steroid hormones are created from cholesterol through enzyme action and this function declines with age. Unfortunately in the cutthroat world of scientific articles you have to sound just as important as everyone else who is trying to sound important which is the reason for the wording of the actual hypothesis. But why, you might ask, the high cholesterol?

Let's look at it from the viewpoint of the body. As we might have implied before, the body can be both brilliant and dumb at the same time. Think of it as having great book smarts but the common sense sometimes gets a bit neglected. You would want an Oxford professor to help you with a bit of math, but you wouldn't necessarily want him on your side in a violent street hooligan brawl after Manchester United loses a football match. So the body looks at steroid hormone levels in the body, and it makes some assumptions.

The main issue is that it isn't feeling too hot because all those steroid hormones are necessary for a lot of different functions and it hasn't quite felt the same ever since they decreased and the dog ran away. Meanwhile, cholesterol is the building block of the body and is responsible for the creation of steroid hormones. At this point the proverbial light bulb turns on above the head and the body starts to hatch a plan together. It puts on the lab coat and goggles (we really wish it wouldn't do that sometimes) and begins to add together what it knows. Hormones are normal and cholesterol is normal, all is fine in the world. Hormones are low and cholesterol is the old normal level, but then why are the hormones low? Ah, but we must make more cholesterol to make up for the deficit!

Yeah, good effort on that one, body. On paper the intentions of the body are just if somewhat misguided. As the body ages, it has trouble putting together all the hormones that it had no issues with earlier in life. So maybe if we increase the cholesterol level, as in increase the raw material so that the finished products can be more readily assembled, then the whole low hormone thing will blow over and become normal again. But as we know, the problem isn't a lack of cholesterol but a breakdown in the enzymatic action that comes about due to age.

Let's think of a city, perhaps in ancient times because back then an overinflated bureaucracy wasn't in charge of city planning. As the city grows to where it wants to be as a city for the purpose it was envisioned, there is ample construction supplies and the workers putting everything in place, building up and maintaining all the construction. Then, slowly over time, the city begins to function at a poor level. Buildings are falling into disrepair, potholes are causing trucks laden with necessary things to swerve off the road to crash and burn, and everything in general is just falling into a sad state. The city, in a panic, orders for more supplies to be made and delivered so that all of these problems can be fixed. Unfortunately nobody took note of the warehouses to see that the necessary supplies are all there. Instead, it seems that there are less workers to take those supplies and to keep the city running smoothly. Maybe the bureaucracy was in charge of city planning after all.

An individual learned in the ways of the world and possessing many different blood tests might at this point say - but my cholesterol is fine and my hormones are still low! This is another hypothesis that we wanted to mention called Relative Hypercholesterolemia. As a quick example, let's look at two individuals, where the levels of "high cholesterol" begin past the 200 mg/dL mark as they do now.

	25 Years old	45 Years old
Julius	140 mg/dL	170 mg/dL
Marcus	170 mg/dL	210 mg/dL
Octavius	189 mg/dL	225 mg/dL
Flavius	150 mg/dL	180 mg/dL

Here we are observing some people, Romans apparently, and how their cholesterol values change as they age. This is a very simple way of looking at relative high cholesterol. Julius and Flavius are doing pretty well, it seems, with both of their cholesterol values being below that dreaded 200 mark. Marcus and Octavius aren't doing as well and any moment now their doctors will probably tell them to lower their cholesterol. But look at the overall comparison for all four people left to right. Everyone's cholesterol levels increased, regardless of the fact that some of them wound up above the threshold or below it. Thus, what we have here is high cholesterol in that it is high "relative" to the point where it originally was when steroid hormone production was peak.

We must also mention the boor ruining the dinner party - low steroid hormone production due to low cholesterol levels, though this particular boor can be influenced by synthetic decreases of cholesterol. Nobody really seems to win at this one. Recall all the negative associations that we have observed with low cholesterol levels and put that into context with not enough building blocks for the production of all those steroid hormones, and things begin to look pretty grim. Certainly grim like the world appears to the multitude of individuals with psychological disorders who have low cholesterol.

Where There's Smoke, There's Fire

Let's take a look at this relative to the definition that we can give cholesterol. Put aside the fact that cholesterol doesn't have a strict definition according to what it is and focus on how we can define cholesterol as it presents itself to the rest of the body. Consider a thermometer. You look at the thermometer and can make some pretty accurate assumptions. It gives you the ability to know if you should go outside and cook some meat on skewers in your shorts or take a big swig of expensive vodka to go break the ice in the lake and swim in your underwear. The thermometer tells us what the actual temperature is outside. We can look at the value of cholesterol in our body both as a rudimentary measuring tool and the units of the actual tool.

However, the thermometer analog doesn't quite cut it with cholesterol. When we look at a thermometer we are asking a question - how hot or cold is it outside? The thermometer answers our question by giving us a value about the actual temperature that is outside, with very little room for error. Also, we apparently have a talking thermometer which is all the rage with kids nowadays. Now let's think about a cholesterol blood test while taking into consideration the link between it and declining steroid hormone production. In fact, let's look at several examples.

Let's say that you get your blood test and say - cholesterol, oh cholesterol, what be thine value? Well, that cholesterol will tell you, no problem at all. Now it is up to you to interpret those numbers. Some people have values of 155, 160, and 170. Based on how we naturally look at it, we would say all those people are fun. Meanwhile, some people have levels of 230, 240, and 245. We would say that those people are not fine. We can say with a great amount of certainty that the last three have disruptions in their steroid hormone production leading to compensation. But what about the first three? All of these individuals could potentially have low steroid hormone production, because while they may be within normal range their levels could be higher than they used to be.

A cholesterol test gives us back the cholesterol value and can possibly tell us something. This something is that because you have high cholesterol, there is a problem in the body. This is the key in understanding this, that high cholesterol is not **the** problem but is rather the **indicator** that there is a problem. Smoke is a way of telling us that something is burning. Let's think for a second and see how this applies to cholesterol lowering drugs. Imagine, if you will, the fire brigade. But instead, they are called the smoke brigade. They don't go around putting out fires. Instead, they go around and make sure that there is no smoke anywhere. Everything is still burning, but hey at least we don't have any of that pesky smoke floating about right? Clearly, one might say that there are a few kinks in such an approach to the prevention of dangerous conditions.

But again, since the body is so complex simple analogs like this don't always cut it. Lowered hormone production has to make do with the cholesterol it is given, and maybe even get a nice buffer from the elevated cholesterol to be able to keep up its steady rate. But what happens when cholesterol lowering drugs are introduced into this equation and take away the cholesterol that is in this delicate and already malfunctioning system? The levels of hormones can possibly drop even further.[37] Let's consider such a situation.

Cholesterol is normal, hormones are normal, but of course then the body has to go and start breaking down. Cholesterol increases to try and make up for lowered hormones but alas, it can only do so much. Cholesterol lowering drugs come into the picture and lower cholesterol so that it looks like everything is alright but hormone levels are still low. But wait, there's more. The cholesterol drugs are liable to be so effective that they may even bring cholesterol down lower than it was before during optimal conditions. Now we find ourselves in what can be termed quite a double whammy situation. The cholesterol level becomes lower than what the steroid hormone production requires, which can result in even lower hormone levels. On top of that, the cholesterol levels from the blood test would seem to imply everything fine when in fact it is even worse. Elevated cholesterol levels are telling us that something is not fully functional in the body, and instead of addressing that problem we are just creating the illusion that everything is fine when it is possibly even worse.

Simply recall the laundry list of side effects we discussed that can arise from the use of cholesterol lowering drugs in Part II. Without having the proper knowledge, one is liable to just think - man those are some pretty strong drugs, but at least my cholesterol is going down. Once a person is adequately aware of the cholesterol-hormone link suddenly the possible list of side effects can explode. On top of statin drug specific side effects, anything that is related to a decline in hormonal levels can also potentially manifest itself as a side effect while using the conventional therapy of cholesterol lowering drugs. We particularly noted statin drugs earlier on because of the way they work, by decreasing the amount of cholesterol by inhibiting an enzyme which is part of the chain towards cholesterol creation (which has the bonus side effect of impacting the links in that chain leading up to the actual cholesterol molecule).

In our own experience of blood test analysis, the lowest hormone levels for the major players are often associated with the use of cholesterol lowering drugs. We would elaborate further on that but after describing the situation as we have, there's really not much to say. The logical chain of events simply reinforces what we have already described. But what about the restorative approach to solving this problem?

Our restorative approach goes hand in hand with what we have described about our program and testing protocol already. A primary force behind our approach is the restoration of steroid hormone levels to help with the issues related to them. It would stand to reason then, that when the restoration of hormones to their optimal levels is achieved, then the elevation of cholesterol should be normalized. Is this another one of those cases of it looking solid on paper but failing in practice? Fortunately not.

In our experience the multi modal approach to the restoration of hormone levels brought with it the normalization of cholesterol levels as well. Note that we specifically mention the normalization of cholesterol and not the lowering of cholesterol. To lower cholesterol is to speak in absolutes about lowering a number which is the indicator and not the true cause. The normalization of cholesterol is achieved by approaching the problem from the logical point - the actual low levels which can cause issues instead of the low levels which show that there are issues.

Hypotheses Need Friends Too

From a logical approach this would all seem to make sense, but that isn't how things work around here. Leonardo Da Vinchi's aerial screw helicopter prototype certainly looked very nice on a piece of aged parchment but it would never actually fly. As good as the logical approach is, the practical approach is the one that ultimately gets results. To that effect we have two published studies that relate some specifics about our approach titled "Hormonorestorative Therapy is a Promising Method for Hypercholesterolemia Management" and "Correction of Steroidopenia as a New Method of Hypercholesterolemia Treatment."[38,39] Let's briefly go through these in order with a summary coupled with commentary to see what happened with extended explanatory comments here and there, starting with believe it or not the first one of the two.

Publication I

In any publication that deals with cholesterol, we certainly can't forget to mention heart disease and how many people die from it. In this case 50% of deaths is that number, which isn't exactly slim pickings.[40-42] Elevation of total cholesterol is of course associated with increased risks of atherosclerosis and heart disease, while a decreased level is associated with a reversion of atherosclerosis in patients with coronary heart disease.[43-46] In the high risk, middle aged population, the treatment of high cholesterol is the most recognized method of keeping atherosclerotic heart disease at bay and many pharmaceutical and treatment methods exist in both North America and Europe.[47,48] However, while the treatment does decrease atherosclerosis, impaired quality of life and side effects are problems.[49,50]

Quality of life adjusted survival is something that as a term is probably not well-known to many, which is a pretty grave oversight. Basically anytime someone is undergoing medical treatment, one has to take into consideration their quality of life. The easiest example is an individual undergoing treatment for something, but being afflicted so severely by the potent side effects that the user is constantly wishing that they were dead instead. You can see where this would be a problem. A doctor certainly doesn't want the patient to feel like he's going to die more from the treatment than from the disease itself.

We noted that recent studies show that while combined androgen and estrogen therapy can decrease total cholesterol, LDL, HDL, and triglycerides and DHEA supplementation alone has been observed to lower total cholesterol and LDL, other studies have failed to confirm such observations.[51-56] One important thing that must be noted here is that such studies usually focus on giving only one dose of a certain agent to the whole population without taking into account the actual goals that should be followed in restoring their hormone levels. Our study involved 112 individuals (34 male, 78 female) with an average age of 54.2 years, with all of them receiving the hormone restoration therapy as outlined in our protocols. The time of observation ranged from 3 months to 12 years. This of course includes such things as cyclical nature where applicable, individualized dosing per initial results, and only bio-identical hormone use.

We mentioned the average age, but as far as the actual range goes the youngest person was 22 and the oldest was 81. All individuals responded to the therapy, with pre-treatment cholesterol average of 252.9 mg/dL dropping down to an average of 190.7 mg/dL which goes with an average reduction of 24.6%. In men this drop was from 268.3 mg/dL down to 188.6 mg/dL (average 29.7%) and in women this drop was from 246.1 mg/dL down to 191.6 mg/dL (average 23.6%). However, let's not speaks solely in numbers. Bar graphs say it better.

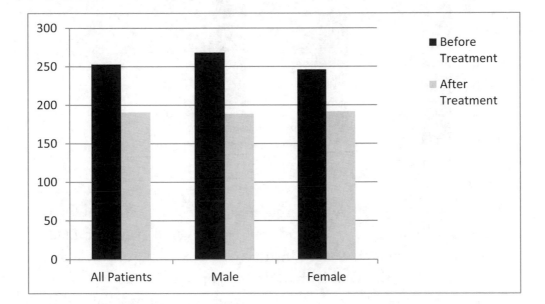

All around HDL levels dropped from 62.7 mg/dL down to 50.1 mg/dL (average 20.1%), but still remained above that minimum lower level of the range. We certainly wouldn't want to decrease something "good" too much, now would we. Women seem to have loaded the dice on this one, because while they saw a decrease of 23.3%, the men only saw a decrease of 3.5%. Again, we can't look at these as "decreases" but rather as normalizations.

If steroid hormone levels are being optimized, there isn't as much cholesterol being produced and not as much excess floating about for HDL to pick up like a police officer making the rounds at college during St. Patrick's Day.

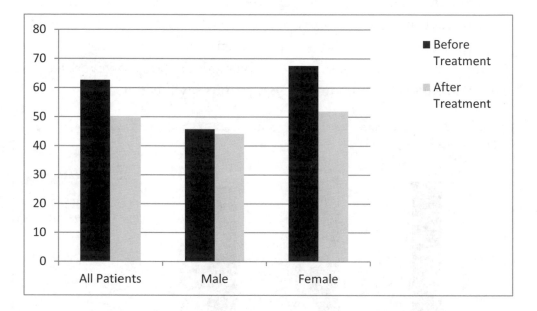

What about the proverbial bad cholesterol. We wouldn't dare forget to look at that as well. The overall drop for LDL levels was from 154.9 mg/dL down to 118.6 mg/dL (average 23.4%). While the women may have won the HDL round, the men come out on top of the LDL. Though we suppose that based on popular perception the men kind of lose here. The drop for men was from 176 mg/dL down to 118.4 mg/dL (average 32.7%) while for women it was from 148.5 mg/dL down to 118.7 (average 20.1%).

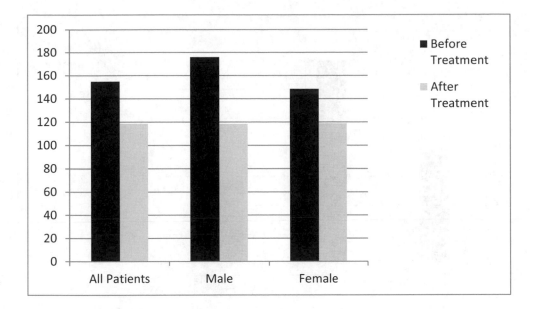

But wait, we are missing a key player. That old brigand triglyceride that we divide by five to estimate the amount of VLDL. The overall drop was from 197.3 mg/dL down to 114.8 mg/dL (average 41.8%). Men, we have good news and bad news. The good news is that you lost more. The bad news is that you lost more because your levels were breaching the stratosphere. While women saw a drop from 144.1 mg/dL down to 104.8 mg/dL (average 27.3%), the men saw a drop from 348.5 mg/dL down to 143.2 mg/dL (average 58.9%).

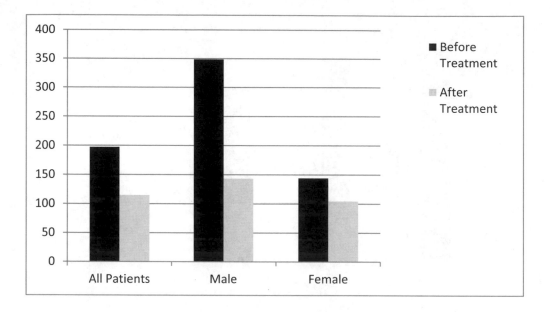

Just look at that towering structure. It almost mirrors the capacity of men to build large objects that are also very tall to penetrate the skies to say one message - a man built this edifice.

The problem with the human body as it ages is the breakdown of balance. No, not a balance that can be divined by following magnetic ley lines within the earth through the attunement of rare crystals, but rather the balance between the creative and destructive. Wow, that doesn't much better than the magnetic ley line thing. Basically, the human body is made to function the best it can when the internal processes that build up, termed anabolic activity, are balanced by the internal processes that break down, termed catabolic activity. The break down process is not inherently bad by a long stretch because it is necessary to remove that which needs to be replaced. However, when you throw age into the equation the problem is that the anabolic starts to get taken over by the catabolic. This normal age related shift of metabolic activity impacts the rate at which age associated disease progress with cardiovascular disease being a good example of such a disease. However, if there is a push to improve anabolic function, then the process of continuous decline can be impeded.

This is important to consider with the overall relation of hormones and cholesterol. There is a great hubbub made about the link between cholesterol and coronary heart disease, but some studies point out that individuals with the "normal" levels of cholesterol experience myocardial infarctions with just as much frequency as those individuals who have high cholesterol. In fact, between 45% and 60% of patients admitted to hospitals for myocardial infarction had cholesterol levels which were within the normal range.[57,58] Our assessment of such situations is that the measurement of cholesterol increases is much more important than an absolute measurement taken at any one time. Seeing how high the level is in relation to previous measurements allows for an observation of the increase of cholesterol which coincides with the decrease of steroid hormone production. This sort of analysis can explain the occurrence of heart attacks in the absence of "high cholesterol."

Our hormone restoration approach once again uses no synthetic hormones, since the latter approach is not as effective. Another key difference is that this is restorative, not replacement. Replacement implies a muscle in approach with a substance that isn't what the body ordered. Restoration is just that, the rejuvenation of what the body is already producing. This replacement approach is part of the issue with synthetic hormone therapy, as well as the lack of dosing in accordance with physiologic values. This sort of rigidity on either or both counts can explain studies with controversial results regarding the use of estrogens, progestogens, androgens, and DHEA in the correction of lipid disorders.[59,60] A DHEA supplementation approach, for example, using traditional means would give the same dose to everyone and see what kind of difference it makes in lipid levels. But what about pre-existing levels, what if the person has great DHEA levels but bad pregnenolone levels, and so on and so forth? This is why the multimodal approach has to be used to ensure results.

Publication II

The focus of the second study is of course also the impact of hormone restoration on cholesterol levels. For our purposes here we can look more at the levels of hormones restored themselves because there is no information in the medical literature about the connection of low steroid hormones with high cholesterol with the exception of a few studies.[61-66] This study was an analysis of 43 individuals who underwent hormone restoration due to hypercholesterolemia with a population consisting of 12 males and 31 females. The average age was 58.4 years, 62.3 for men and 57 for women. The observation period was between three and nine months.

The protocol that was followed for the therapy was again the one that we described, because that is what we actually use. The standards were followed for dose creation in that recommended doses were established via clinical data and hormonal levels, individual doses were always used to bring the level to the optimal range, and the doses used took into account the necessary amount to bring up the levels to the optimal range. The use of hormones followed guidelines as well such as bio-identical hormones only, individually modified doses, larger morning doses, hormone level tests providing adequate data, and multi hormone therapy because a one or two hormone approach is inadequate in the vast majority of cases.

Let's take a look at some hard data here in regards to the cholesterol numbers. The average value of total cholesterol decreased from 228.8 mg/dL down to 183.7 mg/dL (average 19.7%), with values in women decreasing from 229.2 mg/dL down to 186.3 mg/dL and values in men decreasing from 227.9 mg/dL to 177.1 mg/dL (22.3%).

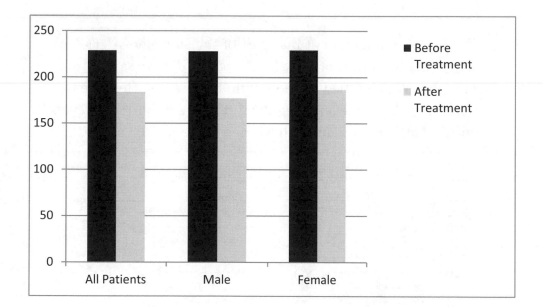

Though the sample population was of small size, all decreases of total cholesterol were statistically significant. We mention statistically significant because if there is one thing that medical studies like to see, it is statistics. We don't want to overload on lipid test bar graphs too much, so we will append a table with the values for the players that made up the total cholesterol values.

All Values are in mg/dL	All Individuals		Women		Men	
	Before	After	Before	After	Before	After
HDL	65.0	53.8	73.3	59.5	43.6	38.8
LDL	137.4	110.2	132.8	109.3	149.3	112.5
Triglycerides	132.7	100.3	115.0	86.7	178.7	135.6

We took a gander at that part of the story, now let's look at some data from the hormone levels. Sorry, did we say no more bar graphs? We specified no more lipid bar graphs. Here are two more graphs, this time showing the difference in hormone levels before and after treatment, with women first and men second.

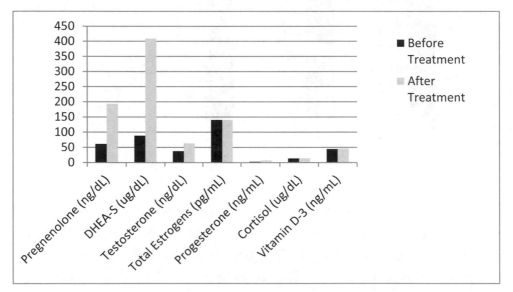

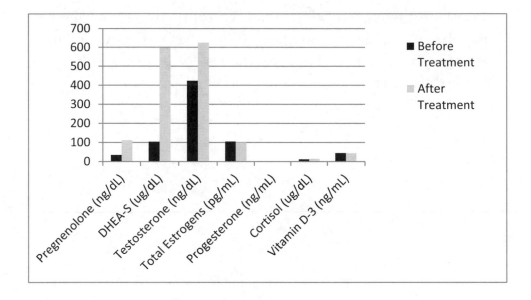

Let's talk about what this means for both genders. For men, hormone restoration lowered total cholesterol apparently by decreasing LDL and triglycerides but without a noticeable difference in HDL. By looking at this statement, we can say that the steroid hormones that are connected to the changes in LDL and cholesterol were DHEA-S, pregnenolone, testosterone and progesterone. Vitamin D-3, cortisol, and total estrogen did not have significant changes. For women, total cholesterol changes were accompanied by decreases in HDL, LDL, and triglycerides, with significant changes in pregnenolone, DHEA-S, testosterone, progesterone, but not for total estrogen, cortisol, or vitamin D-3.

Based on these observations and what we now know about cholesterol, this all seems to make sense. We can follow the steps throughout the creation process of steroid hormones and appreciate everything that goes on. We can use this knowledge to have a second understanding of statin drugs and why they have the potential to cause the harm that they do by cutting off cholesterol production before it is even fully formed. But there may be one lingering question in the back of your mind regarding cholesterol and clogged arteries. We shall cover this in the very next section.

While we certainly can't stave death off for good, we can certainly make the road there a lot less bumpy and put a serious dent in that annual quota.

PART VI

On the Nature of Issues and Disease Related to Physiologic Breakdown

This part is to be the subject of observations and discussion of various breakdowns and diseases. But first, we must follow through with the ending of the previous part and talk about something that we haven't truly yet covered. You know what we are referring to. Even now, it lurks in arteries, building up just ready to cause problems. That nasty, disgusting, yellow, deposit. We just spent so much time trying to remove the tarnish from cholesterol's reputation, but was all of it for naught? Is atherosclerosis going to prove us wrong and bring it all crashing down? Maybe not, and that's another one of those questions we wouldn't ask if we weren't about to do some heavy lifting. Let's take a look at the criminals, shall we?

Atherosclerosis - I Swear Officer, I Was Just in the Area

First of all we can get one thing out of the way, a question, some might say a very important question that is always asked when we speak about disease. What causes atherosclerosis? We don't know. That is to say, nobody knows. How can this be, you might ask. All those commercials, all those charts and diagrams in the doctor's offices, they all mention cholesterol! This is the very important bit that we are often too worried to notice. High cholesterol does not cause atherosclerosis, and any reputable source will make sure to specify this distinction. High cholesterol is at all times associated with atherosclerosis, but nobody can say it causes it because it doesn't. They can say that cholesterol is associated with the atherosclerotic process until the cows come home, because that is a fair statement to make.

While we don't know what actually causes the process to begin that leads to the buildup of atherosclerotic plaque, we do have a good picture of everything that goes into it. Basically, atherosclerosis is the body's response to an in inflammation in the arterial walls via the accumulation of various components. The important bit is that cholesterol is indeed one of these components. When this response happens, LDL is the one that brings it on in to the buildup, while HDL is the one that takes it out of that particular equation. This is ultimately what the terms "good cholesterol" and "bad cholesterol" are referring to, completely misguided and baseless titles as they may be, the intention behind the naming can nonetheless be seen.

Irongut

Macrophages play an extremely large role in the initial development stages of the buildup process. Macrophage may not be a household name, but what a macrophage actually is certainly well-known. A macrophage is a type of white blood cell, the old guard in charge of keeping our body secure against foreign threats. While they can't go outside the body to hunt for germs of mass destruction, they do a very fine job keeping the defensive integrity of our own body in check. The macrophage is also the big boy of the bunch, the biggest white blood cell floating about at a whopping 21 micrometers (10^{-6}). The Greeks don't disappoint again, and the name is very indicative of what it does. Macro referring to big, and phage referring to eating - thus,

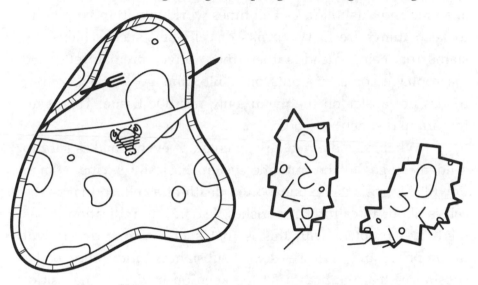

big eater. With a name like that, the criminals of the seedy pathogenic underworld better watch their step as they flee in terror.

The reason that big eater is called as such is because it does exactly that very well. The term for this kind of behavior from this sort of fellow is called phagocytosis, a word when broken down from Greek (what else) roots, goes something along the line of the devouring cell process. We don't mean to cloud your judgment with an image of a cell going to town on a buffet, but rather a process of engulfing certain matter and then absorbing it. Instead of all you can eat taco day at the college food court, imagine a giant mass slowly engulfing something until it is no more and ready to be broken down into the constituent parts. Clearly, a horrific and slow death for pathogens.

However, keeping the home turf clean of rabble rousing invaders is not the only way macrophages use their big appetite to keep the body running. Recall that we mentioned that the anabolic and catabolic are at all times working within your body to keep things fresh. When bits of cells and such achieve the status of being dead rather than alive prematurely, the macrophage comes in, puts on a bib, and goes to work. But there's no lobster on the menu, only necrotic tissue. This is an important distinction to note.

When cells die regularly, a chain of events makes sure to send messages to the immune system basically saying - "man down!" Necrosis is the unexpected death of a cell, so that as the cell is about to call 911 it perishes, leaving no indication it has died. The problem with this is that such necrotic debris will decompose and release toxic substances into the body, substances that the body isn't too keen on having at the risk of grave consequences. Macrophages thus have a very important role in a sort of combined scavenger coroner task.

Macrophages are far from being all stomach and no brains. When the first pathogenic invaders breach the body they are liable to get eaten up, but the process here is far from a simple engulfing and break down. When the pathogen is destroyed, the macrophage acquires a chemical called an antigen, an identifying message of sorts that it got from the actual pathogen, that it sends out to other parts of the immune system. When the rest of the defense force receives this antigen, it begins ramping up production of the proper defensive measures to repel the attacker. This even includes the creation of antibodies that adhere to the invaders to make further phagocytosis easier for the macrophages. In this sense the macrophage is not only an important front line fighter, but even a hybrid general helping your body win the fight.

Eating the dead and keeping the Huns at bay are the more well-known macrophage activities, but there is also a role in creation and rebuilding. When muscle tissue is in need of repair and growth, macrophages come in with a two wave approach. While the first wave is in charge of putting the injured cells out to pasture to make way for new ones, the second wave helps with the regeneration effort.[1-3] However, macrophages are not solely associated with repair of muscle tissue as their accumulation can play a potential role in the repair process in other tissues as well.[4]

No Alibis

What about some of the other perpetrators at the scene of the crime? We already mentioned cholesterol. Calcium is there as well. Surely most of us know about calcium already, as most of the calcium in our body is locked up in our bones and teeth.[5] Though it is also important in areas such as muscle function and nerve transmission, only about 1% of the calcium in the body is used in this way. What is it doing at the site of atherosclerosis?

First we must mention the process of calcification, and not the one giving you inadequate showerhead pressure. In the biological sense, calcification occurs when normally soft tissue is hardened via the accumulation of calcium. How does this apply to atherosclerosis? It occurs in the later stages of atherosclerotic buildup by taking the older already accumulated soft tissue and hardening it, causing it to stay in place. While break offs of atherosclerotic plaque are no walk in the park and can cause some serious complications, imagine if you will what occurs during a process that hardens the buildup that is already starting to block off your arteries. The buildup becomes more entrenched in place, which can give the rest of the plaque buildup process greater coverage to block off more blood flow. This doesn't really look like an all that great function of calcium in this case.

Other lurkers that can show up at the crime scene are thrombocytes, but most of us know them better by their common name of platelets. They are the cell fragments floating around in the blood that are responsible for clotting function. They also have jobs related to homeostasis and cell growth while also being carriers for various substances such as ATP, calcium, and even serotonin. Of course what we care the most about is that when we get cut by a knife wielding football hooligan after their team lost the match is that the platelets will aggregate to the site of injury and work to stop the flow of blood. After all, we prefer for our blood to be inside of our body rather than outside.

Shooting the Messenger

Let's talk on these components of atherosclerosis for a bit. Macrophages, calcium, and platelet. If someone asked you, do you like calcium, how would you answer? Would you say heck no I hate that junk? Odds are you would say that as far as minerals go, calcium is a pretty swell guy. We love calcium. We make sure the children drink milk like water so that their bones grow big and strong. We tell menopausal women to take calcium like breath mints. Everywhere you go, calcium is just great.

What about macrophages? You might not hear much about them or have forgotten since high school biology, but they are very useful. At the very least, how could anyone react negatively to such a useful component of our immune system? And platelets? Why they're the unsung hero of knife fighters and high risk skateboarding teenagers. You can't call a platelet evil, and if you don't have enough of them you will bleed out pretty bad, severely throwing off that whole "blood outside the body to blood inside the body" ratio.

But cholesterol! Man that guy just needs to get out. But wait, we just spent a good bit of time showing that cholesterol is not only a great part of your body, it is absolutely necessary for life. Where are the messages to lower platelets, macrophages, or calcium? Yeah, they're not around. But how is cholesterol different? It is one of the most important parts of your body yet it has such a negative reputation based on association that the other players are just as guilty of having. Recall that cholesterol is brought to sites where it is needed for construction and creation. We don't know what causes atherosclerosis but we can surmise that it is some kind of healing response that goes past well-meaning into "why do you guys want to hurt me."

Based on our assessment of cholesterol being the unsung hero of the body and its relation to hormone production we have a thought here. That catabolic/anabolic ratio keeps on breaking down as we age, and there are many breakdowns that can happen. One such example is the potential for the formation of micro-abrasions in our system of blood vessels. Such miniature "wounds" would be liable to get healed, though as we see in atherosclerosis this doesn't quite work out because it seems like there isn't enough juice in the system to make things right. But recall our earlier mention of HDL functioning like a chameleon, a dirty, shape shifting, possible saboteur. Even the assumed benefits of HDL taking cholesterol out of the atherosclerotic equation can backfire.

But look at all the players of the game. When you fully look at each one individually, you can't say that they are bad. Don't forget that high cholesterol is a result of impaired steroid hormone production, so the lack of hormones certainly isn't helping anything either. High platelets can cause blood clots of the bad kind, and macrophages themselves can be tricked into harboring pathogens like tuberculosis. Even excess levels of calcium can cause constipation or kidney impairment. But are any of these bad as each individual unit based on their overall role in the body? Of course not.

Coronary Heart Disease, an Unbiased Killer

We've already touched on coronary heart disease earlier. We know about some of the modifiable risk factors such as obesity, high blood pressure, smoking, physical activity and so forth. We also know that while cholesterol lowering drugs such as statins can reduce death from the actual disease, overall death tends to stay the same. Last, we know that while surgical procedures such as angioplasties and coronary bypasses can provide relief, they don't add years to the ol' lifespan.

Let's look at one of those risk factors: high cholesterol and by extension low hormones. We've already established that through hormone restoration cholesterol levels can be decreased. But what about the actual role of hormones in this disease other than this overall normalization of cholesterol values to prevent excess cholesterol? We say this because coronary heart disease is generally thought of as a disease targeting primarily men, though this isn't really the case. Cardiovascular disease is actually the leading killer of women, just as it is for men. In fact, women are at higher risk of dying from a first myocardial infarction, having more long term disability, and even a higher risk of displaying additional disease.[6,7] That last bit is also influenced by the fact that women tend to develop this disease later in life than men. Based on our quick run through of the hormones we already saw indicators for optimal muscle function, which the heart certainly is.

Let's take a look at testosterone first, as that is a hormone with such a function. In one study that followed both men and women with angina pectoris (better known as chest pain), it was shown that testosterone supplementation improved the condition for the majority of the population.[8] Another study that alternated taking a placebo with testosterone therapy showed that the therapy showed a marked improvement in angina as well.[9] We're sure the individuals weren't all that happy while taking the placebo, what with the increased chest pain and all.

But this is testosterone supplementation, what about the link between actual low levels of testosterone and heart disease? Luckily there is indeed a link between how low the testosterone levels are compared to the severity of artery blockage in men suffering from coronary heart disease, with the indication being that high levels of testosterone can protect against atherosclerosis.[10] Such studies tend to be focused on men and tend to leave women out in the cold, but all is not lost. The various effects that testosterone has in terms of heart health is analogous to the function estrogen has in women.[11] Even testosterone supplementation itself showed improvements in women with chronic heart failure.[12] Heart failure is certainly bad enough without having the chronic adjective attached to it.

If we are looking at testosterone we should also take a look at DHEA as far as heart health goes. DHEA converts to testosterone, and in women provides a major source of estrogen post menopause. This sort of action increases the appropriate protective levels in both genders. As well as these parts of a restorative approach, antioxidant supplements including the common vitamins E and C as well as the various B vitamins which have been shown to decrease risks of heart attack and even stroke.[13-22]

Andropause, the Bent Weeping Willow, and Grapefruit Prostates

Male impotency. This is a relatively new phenomenon that seems to be afflicting men. Anytime when we look in the past we see evidence that men were manlier. Half naked Greeks holding the line didn't have any testosterone deficiency to speak of, clearly. Certainly our fathers or grandfathers who fought during World War II didn't have any problems. After all, you can't take out Hitler and his Nazi minions when the soldier isn't standing at attention. Obviously this isn't true. The times, they are changing. While great grandpappy was chopping down trees on the frontier and grandpa was fighting the Wehrmacht, there was no time to talk about impotence, because that simply wasn't something to be talked about during the weekly man gathering and pipe smoking.

Nowadays men are bombarded anytime they turn on the television. Commercials frequently come on speaking about the problems of male impotence and what kind of drug can help out. There are even commercials now that tell men that they probably have low testosterone due to aging. Probably is certainly an understatement. Unless a man is an immortal Olympian (or a lobster, we suppose), then his levels will almost certainly decline. As we have said numerous times, this is the way of nature and what happens during aging. Let's not forget flaccid details such as the decrease of almost half of all androgens due to declining DHEA levels, the fact that DHEA levels can fall by up to 74% in the 50s already, and testosterone levels start to approach the bottom of the barrel.[23,24] In fact, 80 year old men have about 15%

of their original DHEA levels, and if they make it to the ripe age of 90, they will have about 5% left.[25] The only stiff thing most men at such an age can look forward to is a stiff neck after spending too much time on the veranda without a scarf during Autumn.

So what about those popular drugs for erectile dysfunction? Basically they work on the concept of - it isn't getting enough blood, fill 'er up. This is partly the reason there are plenty of jokes floating around where men taking such drugs can use their anatomy as a club-like weapon. How is the physiologic side of all this? We can mention several things to reinforce the link.

Men who receive testosterone supplementation have increased sexual potency and viability, which is almost a given.[26] In our experience, the multimodal approach works a might better because testosterone is certainly not the only androgen. Here are some things we want to throw out for your consideration. Average total cholesterol and LDL values were higher in men suffering from erectile dysfunction as opposed to those who weren't.[27,28] Furthermore, high cholesterol is associated with something men don't want to hear anything about - poor testicular function, as well as being found in 65% of infertile men.[29] Here's the special additional bit: two classes of cholesterol lowering drugs, the statins and fibrates, may cause erectile dysfunction.[30,31]

Let's put on our thinking caps. High cholesterol, which can be caused by low hormone production, is associated with erectile dysfunction. Statin drugs, which lower cholesterol values, the same cholesterol that steroid hormones are made from, may cause erectile dysfunction. Not enough testosterone naturally, or not enough testosterone due to a decrease in the building block that creates testosterone. If high cholesterol was the cause of erectile dysfunction, lowered cholesterol should logically fix this problem, yes? We'll just leave it at that to talk about the other bit now.

Andropause. Men might not be as familiar with it, but it is certainly happening. There is some contention about the concept of a menopause analogue in men because while a menopausal woman loses her ability to reproduce, a male does not necessarily. One could always argue that a man is only as viable in reproduction as his ability to get a soldier to stand up straight and deliver the armaments, but we digress. A major fear of aging men is the thought that the now frequent trips to the bathroom are either from what feels like a melon sized prostate or a cancer attacking a source of their manhood. Either scenario isn't very nice.

Prostate cancer is no friend of man, or anyone for that matter. A common notion is that testosterone can cause this situation to get outright dire, which nobody wants to happen. However, it appears that low testosterone seems to actually increase the risk of acquiring prostate cancer as well as having an association with more aggressive prostate cancer.[32,33] Men often wish that their favorite athlete is more aggressive in their respective sport, but under no circumstances do they wish for their prostate cancer to be of the aggressive sort. High testosterone levels are associated with decreased prostate cancer risk, and high levels prior to the occurrence of prostate cancer resulted in improved survival rates.[34,35]

Menopause, the End of Monthly Visits

This and andropause are the reason we specifically titles this part as being "issues" and not just disease. Certainly men don't want to think of their erectile dysfunction as a disease, though it is, just as we can say with menopause. Again, we have to look back at the root meaning of disease and remember that it is broader than the terms of the Treaty of Tordesillas. That is to say, it covers quite a lot. It can be an infectious affliction, but it can also be anything that is a breakdown of the "normal condition." We still won't call menopause disease because it sounds a bit off, but we can certainly say that functionality is greatly impaired.

After all, not only is menopause the signaling of the end of having to worry about birth control, but it is also the time associated with all those things that we consider linked to menopause. But of course you, vested in the garments of basic biological know how, understand that a major part of menopause is the major decrease in the levels of estrogens and progesterone. Let's recall our earlier description of the monthly cycle. It looks something like this.

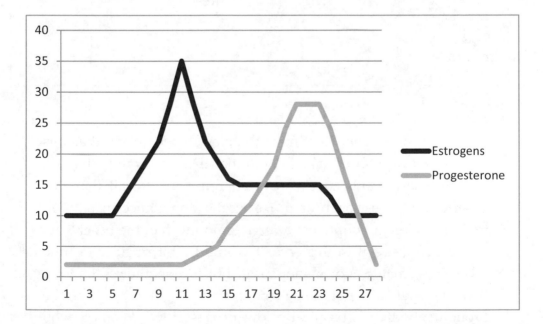

This is the way that the monthly fluctuations of these hormones goes down (don't pay too much heed to the numbers on the y-axis, they are there to provide a good indicator of the ups and downs of the cycle). However, when menopause moves into town, it puts a stop to this "balanced" nonsense and institutes a new rule for the ratio of estrogen and progesterone. This is what it looks like.

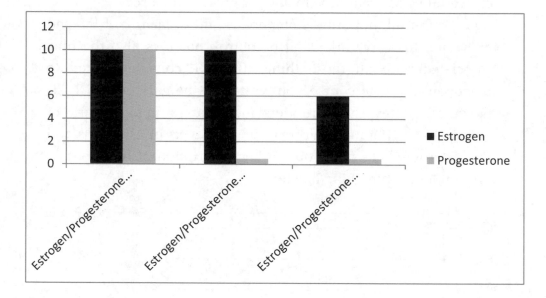

Certainly you don't have to be an expert to see that this isn't so hot. It is important to note that these are ratios that are not necessarily indicative of overall numbers. Recall that our descriptions of estrogen or progesterone dominance in no way implies a large amount, just a *larger* amount than the other guy, or we suppose gal in this case. The middle bit refers to a time when a woman is not menopausal, but is nonetheless infertile because eggs are not being released. Such an issue can be brought about by chronically low progesterone. Women who have trouble conceiving and keeping early pregnancies are often given progesterone as part of the fertility treatment. As for the menopausal ratio, we can simply refer back to our deficiency and dominance charts for estrogens and progesterone.

When a woman is in her prime, things are generally going well on account of a good balance between the hormones. But then, the balance is inevitably broken. Issues can arise from the standard gallery of symptoms related to low levels of progesterone, estrogen, and as the case frequently may be, estrogen dominance. We simply have to refer back to our listings to see some of the bedlam that can arise from this imbalance: fatigue, weight gain, hot flashes, hair loss, headaches and migraines, depression, uterine fibroids, fibrocystic breasts, well we could be here for a while listing. A refresher of symptoms is back in Part IV.

Post-menopausal women are certainly no stranger to hot flashes. In fact, many women experience these frustratingly hard to diagnose occurrences well before menopause due to the lack of optimal hormonal balance. Nobody would deem to say that hot flashes are a mild event, lest they get punched by an angry woman, but it is certainly possible to say that in the grand scheme of things hot flashes are not all that vile when compared to the likes of ovarian and breast cysts. These cysts associated with low progesterone levels are no walk in the park, and neither are cancers of the same variety.

All these issues are caused by the lack of balance as well as the deficiency of hormones. Upkeep of this balance can have a very good prognosis on the issues that can occur due to the lack of the protective buffer afforded by both balance and higher levels. Furthermore, restoration of levels closer to the ones found earlier in life can greatly help with such nagging issues as part of the multimodal approach.

Migraine - Alas Poor Brain!

You might ask why did we append this right after menopause and issues related to "female hormone" imbalance. If you have to ask this question, then you are probably a man. Unfortunately, while women get the improved life expectancy compared to men, one of the offsets is that women are afflicted by migraine with much higher frequency. Migraine is a bit like atherosclerosis. Atherosclerosis clogs your arteries and nobody knows why, whereas migraine hurts like the Dickens and nobody knows why. That's right - science doesn't fully understand string theory and what exactly causes migraine.

However, while we don't exactly know what causes it, many people are familiar with its effects. Anyone who refers to a migraine simply as a "bad headache" is probably blessed with mild migraine or has never experienced one, and we would lean towards the latter reason. Many migraine sufferers experience various indicators that signal the onset of migraine and even have to stay away from certain dietary triggers. The only thing worse than getting migraine is not being able to eat New York cheesecake because it can set the migraine off. More than a few individuals even get what is termed an aura shortly before the onset of migraine. Unfortunately getting an aura refers not to the procurement of mystical powers but instead to visual events or impairments ranging from bright, flashing white or multi colored lights, blurred vision, and even zigzagging patterns across the field of view.

The actual migraine pain ranges from severe to having the brain feel like Julius Caesar after realizing he was surrounded not by friends but dirty conspirators. On top of these murderous pains several associated events can occur such as nausea (a very common side event), diarrhea, or blurred vision to mention a few. Another very common side event with migraine that can last for a decent bit is sensitivity to light and sound, which is why many migraine sufferers retreat to a dark room and lie down. The lying down part because migraine is also often debilitating, because clearly all the other issues weren't already enough. For people who suffer severe chronic migraine, the combination of all these issues can modify existing calendars not based on 28-31 days, but rather on days split down the middle between functional days and "I feel like a vampire lying on the couch in a dark room the whole time" days.

All that aside, here are some very interesting parts. Interesting from a scientific standpoint of course, not in the amount of grief they cause the sufferer. A big "migraine risk factor" is menstruation.[36] Another interesting bit is that while boys and girls suffer about the same rates of migraine pre-puberty, after the fact the ratio starts to take on the woman biased one we know and hate. In fact, migraine occurrence and overall patterns are influenced by factors such as the first menstruation that a woman experiences in her life, the use of oral contraceptives (laden with hormones, of course), pregnancy, perimenopause, and menopause.[37]

What is a common thread in all these things? The fluctuating levels of progesterone and estrogens, as if we haven't thrown enough charts at you to reinforce that fact already. This is where the restorative approach comes in. While we can't say definitively what precisely causes migraine same as everyone else, we can certainly say a large part of it seems to be around an imbalance of various physiologic factors. This is based on our own experience with women afflicted with migraine who are on the restorative program.

What we have to stress here is that simply trying to optimize the levels and balance of progesterone and estrogens is not nearly enough. While they seem to play a large role overall in the equation, the use of all the hormones such as pregnenolone, DHEA, and even testosterone have been shown to be variably effective across different individuals. This is always made challenging in what is both the greatest asset of the physiologic approach and the greatest challenge: no two individuals react the same way, because no two people's bodies break down in the same way. While the overall approach works in many cases and shows great promise, it has to first reach that point by starting out on a semi common ground and then narrowing down the specifics.

Other factors seem to play into the treatment of migraine as well. A pretty significant one at times seems to be the use of magnesium and the optimization of the balance between magnesium and calcium. Adequate levels of important neurotransmitters such as serotonin and melatonin can also play a large role. Even the restoration of impaired intestinal flora seems to play a role in certain cases, as well as a preliminary parasitic cleanse to flush out potential infestation. The last thing we need in our bodies is parasitic worms defecating in our homeostatic establishment.

When that perfect assemblage of agents is collected from the individualized approach along with a good dose of that old brigand trial and error, migraine is often greatly decreased in severity or even altogether gone. In the interim even particularly painful and long lasting episodes of migraine can be controlled by an extra addition of the items already used, the proverbial restorative torch in the woods at night against the migraine wolves.

Fibromyalgia, Not Pleasurable in the Least Bit

Fibromyalgia is another one of those fiendish afflictions targeting mostly women and having no straight known cause, just like migraine. While migraine affects women in a 3:1 ratio compared to men, fibromyalgia hits harder with a ratio of 9:1.[38,39] Fibromyalgia can basically be described as chronic and widespread pain, and the extra salt in the wound is that stimuli that previously did not cause pain can do so. Let's look at some associations and how they can factor into the restorative approach.

A hypothesis is floating about that fibromyalgia may be due to an irregular disturbance of the neural, immune, and endocrine systems.[40] The endocrine system is responsible for hormone production, the neural system is obviously in charge of the nerves, which hormones play a large role on, and the immune system can also be impacted in large part by the hormones. This is a hypothesis that we can throw our hats off to because fundamentally it appears to make sense since our experience with the restorative approach has been used to help women suffering from fibromyalgia.

Fibromyalgia has been associated with a delayed onset of menstruation for girls and with infertility in women, both of which we can associate with hormonal imbalance.[41] Fibromyalgia suffers have some symptoms such as fatigue, poor sleep, and psychological problems which can be associated with hormonal deficiency as well.[42] Disorders such as migraine, panic disorders, irritable bowel syndrome, chronic fatigue syndrome, and major depression occur frequently with fibromyalgia, which seems to imply an underlying connection.[43] Furthermore, migraine, fibromyalgia, irritable bowel syndrome, and other such related conditions exhibit common patterns across a variety of systems.[44-47] Let's finish this one off strong and mention that a possible cause of fibromyalgia appears to be an overly excited central nervous system.[48]

Think back to our earlier discussions - anytime a steroid hormone is known for one thing, it winds up either being a neurosteroid or having very beneficial action towards neural action. We may weave a complex web with our narration, but hopefully it all links back to the center in your mind. Recall that a primary function of neurosteroids is controlling how excitable neurons can be. Finally, we can mention the straight up neurotransmitters in their apparent roles with fibromyalgia. The disease is associated with inadequate "deep sleep" and sleep that doesn't do its proper job and leave one feeling refreshed.[49,50] Suffers have been observed to have low melatonin levels and supplementation of melatonin for individuals with fibromyalgia resulted in reduced pain, sleep issues, and depression.[51]

Relating to Afflictions of the Joints and Bone

Let's talk about arthritis, or more specifically rheumatoid arthritis and osteoarthritis. While we're here we might as well throw in osteoporosis, though it isn't quite in the same ballpark. On the subject of arthritis, most of us are familiar with it, if not personally then probably knowing at the very least one individual who has it. As a basic definition, we can call arthritis an inflammatory disorder relating to the joints. The ones we specified are certainly not the only ones out there, just the ones we will be mentioning here, because there are over one hundred different types of arthritis. Let's talk about rheumatoid arthritis first, and because that is a pain to write out and say each time, we will call it RA.

RA is a long term inflammatory disorder that can affect not only the flexible joints, but even other organs as well. Recall our earlier discussion about the immune system meaning well but being a bit overeager in its function, leading to inflammation. RA is like the poster child of that. What begins as a short trip down Inflammation Avenue eventually leads to buying permanent living quarters in Joint Immobility and Deformity City (what a terrible name for a town). Other unpleasant occurrences include the growth of nodules on the skin, rheumatoid lung disease, and kidney damage.[52,53] Cherries on top of the autoimmune cake include high risks for atherosclerosis, myocardial infarction, and stroke, as well as an increased risk of lymphoma.[54-57]

Seeing as this is primarily an autoimmune disease, optimized physiologic function can certainly benefit here. Various steroid hormones work on the immune system to provide the best functionality and defense, as well as modulating the severity and fervor of response. Individuals on the restorative program can have improved symptoms and functionality, though the point of progression of RA can be an impediment in this.

What of osteoarthritis? This one is actually the most common form of arthritis and is the age related, wear and tear format and is also the most common form of chronic disability in the United States.[58,59] Basically, imagine if you will, all the joints and the bones that are connected in this manner in your body. Now imagine said joints wearing away through the reduction of the actual cartilage as well as the degradation of the end points of the bones that are attached. The concept of bones grinding on bones is perhaps more painful to think about than recalling what nails going down chalkboard sound like.

The common conception is the ol' you're getting old excuse, along with other factors such as a long life full of use and factors such as being overweight or having injuries. We certainly can't disagree with this, but can't help but notice that this isn't the whole picture here. What happens during aging? A decrease of hormone of course, as if we haven't mentioned that enough yet. Certain hormones such as testosterone and estrogen play important roles in bone health. Estrogens alone are a big factor in the balanced ratio of bone breakdown to bone buildup, and is responsible for keeping adequate amounts of collagen present in the human body - collagen being a primary building block of cartilage. As for the bone itself, don't neglect to remember that the end points of the bone also become worn out, so the integrity of the bone structure is compromised as well.

With this we piggyback onto osteoporosis and find that we don't actually have much to say. When we spoke about estrogen and its hormonal benefits we already spoke about the destructive and creative process of bone. Throwing calcium at the problem is only half the battle and as a single mode approach not necessarily the best way to go about it. A big part of osteoporosis in the view of the restorative approach is as always the preventative aspect, since if estrogens and other steroid hormones are maintained the likelihood of an imbalanced buildup and destruction ratio are much less.

Macular Degeneration, Ocular Occlusion

Macular degeneration is better known as Age-Related Macular Degeneration, which is then further better known by its acronym AMD. It is also the number one cause of blindness in older adults. Without getting too far into the medical nitty gritty of it all, macular degeneration is the degeneration of the macula (we know what you're thinking, it was a surprise to us as well). The macula, a part of the retina, contains a large concentration of cells that can convert oncoming light into signals, thus playing a large part in our high resolution colored vision. What this means functionally ranges from blurred vision to loss of central vision, and other impairments such as shadows and trouble discerning contrast. The problem here is that unlike bad vision, putting on a pair of glasses won't help in this case.

Macular degeneration can be further subdivided into dry and wet forms. If you think that doesn't sound very "sciencey" then you would be correct. The dry variant refers to central geographic atrophy while the wet form refers to neovascular or exudative macular degeneration. Dry and wet don't sound too bad now, do they? Basically dry refers to the atrophy of cells under the retina, leading to vision loss, while wet refers to abnormal blood vessel growth which can ultimately leak (we apologize for that mental image) and cause damage to the light catching cells and some serious vision loss if untreated. Dry can in fact transform into wet, though this is not common.

Enter drusen. These oddly named accumulations begin to... accumulate in the macula during macular degeneration and are composed in part of cholesterol. If you thought, "why what is that handsome devil doing here, is he on a mission of restoration and rebuilding," then we would raise our hands in expectation of a slow motion high five. Though improvements linked to slowing down or stopping macular degeneration (perhaps even reversing) via the restoration of steroid hormones already look promising, macular degeneration is a bit of a slow mover so this will take time to properly observe. A particularly good complementary and already recognized beneficial treatment strategy is the use of various nutrients and antioxidants. There is already a large amount of carotenoids in the macula as well.

Stem Cells and Hormones, a Bold Alliance

More like, a necessary alliance. Due to media attention, we're certain that most people are at least familiar with stem cells, so we will simply define them as progenitor cells that can turn into whatever cells the body requires. It is an all in one cell that has both the means and the blueprints to become whatever it needs to become. One would say, a useful cell. We won't dwell on the commotion associated with stem cell therapy and leave that to the politicians, because as we're sure we can all agree, politicians know everything about everything. Specifically from our point of reference here, we will be speaking on stem cells harvested from your own body.

Basically, stem cells can function to rejuvenate and repair the body, which can be greatly aided by well-functioning metabolic activity. What has great control over metabolic activity? Hormones. Our reasoning is that for stem cell therapy to be optimal on all fronts, optimized hormones must also follow in tow or already be present. What about the link between hormone and stem cells?

First we should mention the big players in all this - bone marrow stem cells. Studies show that stem cells from the bone marrow can become cells as varied as neurons, cardiac muscle cells, skeletal muscle cells, and even the cells that line our blood vessels.[60-62] As is easily evident in this variety, stem cells can do quite a bit in restoring the functional body.

DHEA leads the charge with benefits such as increasing the growth rate of human neural stem cells and the proliferation of progenitor cells.[63,64] Progesterone has many receptors in certain types of stem cells and is a key player in the defense and upkeep of the nervous system and spinal cord.[65-68] Testosterone has the potential to increase progenitor cells in the bone marrow as well as inducing and furthering the differentiation of embryonic tissue.[69,70] Suffice to say, there is plenty to be said between the major controllers in our bodies and cells that can become what we need most.

We bring this up because while stem cell therapy is an extremely promising field in concept and already in practice, side effects from the transplants can occur. Such issues include lowered hormone levels such as testosterone and estrogens, impaired menstrual cycles, and adrenal insufficiency. Stem cell therapy also currently has co-treatment regimens which include steroids and other such pre and post plans, the side effects of which can be alleviated with hormone restoration.

Regarding Other Villains at the Breakdown Theatre

Here we will mention in passing certain impairments or diseases where we can associate or potentially associate improvements based on the restorative, physiologic approach. The brevity inherent here is primarily because it is simply a refresher of what we have already mentioned earlier on within the context of restorative medicine.

Of Madness and Melancholy

Madness is perhaps a very strong word to use here, but one can never underestimate the impact that an optimized physiology can have in staving off what might seem like unlikely issues. After all, we simply have to remember that low cholesterol is associated with violent crime, of all things.[71] Throughout this narrative we have been reinforcing the fact that steroid hormones have many functions associated with the neural realm and the proper function therein. Recall that impaired steroid hormone levels are associated with anything from anxiety disorders to depression, while optimal levels or supplementation seem awash with benefits. Even Parkinson's, a serious neural impairment, is affected by hormones. We can certainly never forget the link between low cholesterol levels and suicidal tendencies.[72,73]

Insomnia, Land of 1000 Tosses and Turns

The causes of insomnia are far and varied. We might be worried about that meeting tomorrow, if we are going to purge our bowels tomorrow from eating at that roadside taco stand for dinner, or perhaps we are concerning ourselves with rising gas prices. Counting sheep is hard to do when we can't afford to fill up our tank to go to the pasture. However, outside of strictly "worry" insomnia, there are a lot of physiologic factors associated with insomnia such as fibromyalgia, migraine, psychological issues, and the list goes on. A good balance of the important neurotransmitters and hormones can help with this potentially pretty serious issue, be it purely mental on our part or due to deep physiologic issues. We mustn't neglect to mention melatonin, the neurotransmitter that is basically in charge of our biological clock.

Type II Diabetes - What Kind of Sick Person Baked All These Delicious Cookies?

Diabetes is certainly not only about being barred from all manner of confectionary delights. Nobody is going to be thinking about a lack of cake eating when poor circulation leads to the amputation of a beloved body part. On further thought, all body parts would be beloved when taken in the context of amputation. Physiologic optimization is a complex process with many functions and key players, a major component of which is of course hormones. As far as the link with hormones, we simply have to remember the big picture of hormones as metabolic controllers. Low testosterone levels have been observed in men with type 2 diabetes and are associated with increased insulin resistance.[74-76] Insulin resistance is the one you don't want to build up, because that is part of the diabetes play book. Testosterone supplementation has actually been shown to decrease insulin resistance.[77] One bit of word play that can sometimes trip people up is the improvement of insulin resistance. The improvement of insulin resistance is the decrease, not the increase. We want to steer clear away from increased insulin resistance. Another of the hormones, progesterone, plays an important role in the release of insulin and function of the pancreas (where insulin is produced, believe it or not).[78]

No, I Prefer Being Bald and I Love Hats

While some men look like action heroes and grizzled gladiatorial pit fighters when they go bald and shave off the rest, many other men would rather not part with their hair, thank you very much. We've already established that increased DHT is the body's well-meaning effort to make up for decreased testosterone. The irony is lost on the body that by trying to increase the potency of testosterone function in men it is hampering efforts at improving reproductive viability at the local bar. Cortisol would like to remind us that it too can play a hand in this with chronically low or high levels.

Our Intimate Intestinal Friends

Surely we remember that a proper amount of the beneficial bacteria that populate our intestines is essential to our good health. The bulk of serotonin present in the body resides here, and even issues such as irritable bowel syndrome seem to be linked through biological cahoots with the likes of migraine and fibromyalgia. Indeed, the connections to our nervous system and our digestive system are many. This may sound like a silly notion but recall the last time you tried to do anything on an empty stomach. Yeah, the stomach isn't going to have any of that and will make sure that you are well aware that the mighty glutton requires sustenance before he lets the brain do any serious thinking. A healthy digestive system is key to a healthy body. On this note, we can move on to the final part.

When Bacchus isn't gorging himself on fine wines and foods, he probably isn't worrying about his cholesterol.

PART VII

On the Nature of Nutrition and Health

Nutritionist, hedge wizards, celebrities losing weight on the television, diet aids... one might go a bit insane trying to keep track of all the "healthy eating" and weight loss advice that we are subject to. There is certainly enough of it floating about there. What about the restorative approach to medicine? Where does weight loss and diet fit in there? We have certainly spoken about obesity as a risk factor in a great multitude of ailments, because it is, but we haven't specifically spoken how restorative medicine seeks to make us lose weight.

This is because weight loss has to be approached from many directions. One could say that the battle against obesity is as multimodal as restorative medicine itself. Let's consider, for a second, our greatest enemy - fat. We go to great lengths to mention how the body doesn't particularly like to create things that are bad for it, it just might happen here and there if there is a breakdown in function. Fat is an excellent asset in our body. It helps us dissolve vitamins that are only soluble in fat and would thus be unavailable to us if it wasn't for our weight bearing friend. Fat is an exceptional storage unit of calories, setting aside excess so that it may be employed for possible future lean times. It is even a buffer against disease, keeping us healthy longer and giving us an edge in the fight against foreign invaders. That's all great and all, but fat is also keeping us out of our size 30 jeans, so how do we get rid of it?

The restorative approach seeks to make sure that everything is working in fine order. Recall how the balance between progesterone and estrogen can help with fat accumulation. Think back to how testosterone helps build muscle and keep fat content down. DHEA is increased with exercise, and it is just the little engine that could do everything it wants to because boy is it powerful. But is this optimized body, checked up and good to go, going to lose all your weight? Yes and no. A big, obese, resounding no.

Everyone to Blame

Think back to your last outing amongst the general populace. Depending on if you live in Colorado or Mississippi and the population of your locale, odds are that you saw some obese children, maybe some obese teenagers, and perhaps even some obese 20 to 30 year olds. If you think through the context of the restorative approach and all that you have found out about optimized steroid hormones and how well the body metabolism works at a younger age, you might think what in the world is going on here? Aren't all these fine specimens of youth and virility supposed to look great?

Of course they're not. An individual is going to look as physically fit as he or she decides to be. In our modern westernized society we have many scientific advances, perhaps one of the most convenient being the drive through fast food joint. We aren't even remotely going to implicate ourselves as a fast food nation chained to our delicious burger overlords. Is fast food by nature and widespread practice unhealthy? Yes it is. Should they always have healthier menu options and alternate choices? Sure, if they want to. But is anyone holding a gun to anyone's head to go to said fast food places? We certainly hope not, because that is a very strange kidnapping.

Ok, so fast food places are a given as a generally "unhealthy" choice of eating. What about restaurants? Surely there is a wide variety there. Why, there are even ones tailored for the health minded individual, serving up all sorts of foods ranging from delicious to maybe edible, depending on the locale and one's inclination. But those portions, oh those portions. The value for a great meal in the United States and many other countries approaches the astronomical of values in many eateries. You might pay in the range of 11 to 20 dollars and get a heaping portion of food masterfully prepared to satisfy all our darkest desires for great food. Is it going to be good? Most certainly. Is it going to be too much? Yeah, pretty much.

This is one of the biggest issues in weight gain because it is so insidious. We don't even have to specifically think of restaurants, but certainly do because the ante is greatly increased there. If we go out for a nice meal, our psychology is going to want to hoard that meal and finish it to the bone. We don't need doggy bags for our leftovers, we went out for a good cooked meal and we're going to enjoy it. We are out of our home, we procured a cooked meal, and our brain is going to say go for it. Our hunter and gatherer ancestors will be proud. Unfortunately, this type of mentality starts to transfer into other parts of our life.

Take a nice meal that for all practical intents and purposes we can define as "healthy." Now make it a heaping portion. The food is still healthy and good, but that extra portion is what truly kills it. It doesn't matter how healthy it is, if we become either full or get approximately all the calories our body think it might need, all the leftovers are going to get stored in the best way possible: fat. For our size 30 jeans, this is probably something that we want to avoid.

So what about all this - do we suggest any sort of diets as part of the restorative approach? No. Diet is from the Greek word *diaita*, which doesn't mean an altered way of eating. *Diaita* means way of life, which means not only choosing whether we eat the carrot or that delicious double stacked burger, but also how much physical activity we do and of course in general how healthy we live our lives. The human palate is as varied as can be, and eating habits of individuals are vastly different. It is up to

the individual to take the responsibility of eating less as needed and not making bad calls like that amazing double burger with all those extra sides, or like that delicious cheese cake from the nearest grocery store bakery (hey whatever, each small slice is only 500 calories). This is a big part of losing weight in conjunction with the restorative approach. While we can't attest that a carrot can win in a no holds barred street fight, it certainly wins in nutritional value.

If we optimize our hormones and then don't change our eating habits then why should we expect to lose any weight? We can't. Our body is a master at watching out for itself. If we uphold the status quo in dietary intake then our body is going to take it as a green light for not doing anything and keeping that excellent emergency store of fat in reserve. This is the part where the other bit starts to come into play: physical activity.

Who Says Leg Warmers Went Out of Style?

This is of course that dreaded physical activity. When our body demands that we get up off the couch from our Ngorongoro Crater wildlife marathons on the television and says that we need to move around. The impetus for not letting our gym membership go to waste on account of 2 out of 28 days used in February. Caloric reduction can be slow, so exercise has to be increased to help pick up the slack. While many might blame sedentary behavior on the American lifestyle, some people seem to lack perspective.

Imagine the old world, as it were, the old Europe, all that good stuff. Now imagine millennia and centuries of dirty barbarians fighting over land, then some slightly more enlightened barbarians establishing castles and some cities here and there, and then some more fighting but at the core built up from those initial forays. An era of horses, oxen, and peasants. Countless towns and cities grew from a very early start, historically speaking when mentioning the age of places where people live. This layout helped facilitate a "walking distance" thought process. As technology improved, public transportation plugged up the holes and many things remained walking distance. Meanwhile, in America, things were different.

The planning of a majority of American cities outside the New England metropolitan area was built with distance and space in mind. Happy go lucky Swedes biking in their mild weather have to only spend a couple of days in Mississippi in the summer traveling 15 miles to the closest grocery store, where breathing is akin to having a wet rag over the mouth and nose while heatstroke lurks by every magnolia tree, to see the dilemma that we can face. You might say, but what about all those countries near the equator with all those skinny people? We would mention that the nation of Kuwait is actually more obese than America, and one would certainly say it gets quite hot there.[1]

That's the point - we can't blame the weather, large distance making car travel necessary outside of certain metropolitan areas, and sweet, blessed air conditioning for our wave of obesity. We aren't saying that we should start biking because that's ridiculous, how else are we going to fit all these groceries and snack cakes that we bought on the back of a bike? The overall point is that any physical activity is better than no physical activity.

That is all that we can recommend when it comes to weight loss. The optimization of physiologic function can certainly improve energy and vigor, also known as those things necessary to allow us to not die in the gymnasium, but that is only 25% of the equation. The rest has to be filled in by each individual according to his or her abilities. We can only suggest these non-specific bits of advice in regards to losing and keeping off weight because the specifics are completely up to each person.

There is another thing that anyone taking the restorative approach needs to watch out for. Improvement of metabolic activity means the optimization of the anabolic and the catabolic to hopefully what they were at a younger age. This optimization can also potentially mean that the body is up to its old tricks in being able to compartmentalize all the food that we eat better than we might remember. Optimized intestinal flora may be able to better access those calories it might have been missing out on during depleted manpower and the adrenal hormones can push the body into creation mode, but without any activity to coincide with this creation mode the extra effort can go to squirreling away food again. Body, you should really stop while you're ahead.

Eating Our Greens (and Oranges)

As children, we are told to eat our vegetables. As adults, we are told by people who look more fit than us that we have to eat healthy. But what exactly does that mean? Why are we encouraged to eat our "greens" and all that food when there is so much steak out there to be consumed? Besides, the cows eat the greens, we eat the cows, and everything is good right? If it were only so. What we will do now is to provide not specific eating advice, but rather some illumination what it really means to "eat healthy."

If questioned, many individuals who suggest for others to eat healthy will simply say that to eat healthy is to eat healthy, what do you mean what do I mean? At this point many would be tempted to punch the person, and we wouldn't necessarily disagree with that. But what is it that makes that cauliflower good, or that carrot beneficial? Again, we aren't going to tell you what to eat. It is a given that the 500 calorie a slice cheesecake is not the wisest option. What we will do is run through a brief list of those vitamins, what they can do, some examples of where they can be found in good quantities, and exactly why they are important based on their functional role within the body. This is also not meant to be an exhaustive list, simply one displaying some of the benefits of what is in those fabled "healthy" foods.

Antioxidants, Defending Us From What Makes Us Live

That might certainly be a strange title, but such is the nature of antioxidants. We hear about these all the time, and that they're good for us, but what exactly are they? This is one instance where we can turn to the English language, and not the Greek, to help us out. If you can read this, then you already know what anti means. Great, that's covered. An oxidant is referring to something which oxidizes. So an antioxidant is naturally something which prevents the oxidation of another molecule. Let's go further in depth with that.

An oxidation reaction can release free radicals, and these molecules can wreak havoc on cells. So why do we have these oxidation reactions? Because we breathe in oxygen. Unless you are an obligate anaerobe (congratulations on your literacy, by the way), then you need to breathe in oxygen to live. An easy example of oxygen is in the electron transport chain, which is how we get out energy. Without oxygen, we don't just lose function, we lose life.

However, because oxygen is so reactive (if there is nothing to bind to it binds to itself in the form of O_2), it can cause unwanted damage to our cellular structure, including even proteins, lipids, and DNA.[2] We might remember DNA as the keeper of our genetic material, so we certainly don't want that to be damaged. Basically antioxidants fight the good fight by preventing the oxidant from getting out of hand and roughhousing around in our body. Unfortunately for the antioxidant, this means that it itself gets oxidized. Well, at least it isn't us. We salute you, brave antioxidant, now go die for your motherland. For our purposes here we won't mention common foods that you can find antioxidants for two reasons. One is that the body produces antioxidants on its own such as uric acid, and we certainly don't advocate cannibalism. Second is that some of the major dietary antioxidants are vitamins which we will be looking at and noting what foods contain them, reducing unneeded redundancy.

Where to find them: Vitamin E, C, Beta Carotene, Ubiquinol, Zinc, Selenium.

Vitamin A

When we talk about Vitamin A in foods, we are speaking about either retinol, which is vitamin A found in animals that we eat, or carotenes, which are for the most part found in the plants that we eat. The popular recognized role of vitamin A is in regards to vision, to which it is vital. Retinal (not retinol) is the form of vitamin A which allows us to see. As you can see, it is somewhat important. It has important functions in skin health and can help with issues such as acne, psoriasis and skin cancer.[3] It is also an important regulator of the immune system and can even help keep out viruses and bacteria by making the skin and mucous membrane better barriers against these party crashers.[4-8]

Deficiency of vitamin A might immediately go to vision impairment and this is certainly part of it. Deficiency can make it hard or impossible to see in low light (night blindness) and lead to damage in the cornea and retina, two important parts of the eye (are there any unimportant parts of the eye), which can contribute to blindness.[9] Pointing out that vitamin A is an important part of the immune system naturally leads to serious issues when there is a deficiency. Deficiency can lead to impaired infection combat and death due to complication from infectious disease in children.[10] Deficiency can also lead to more instances of pneumonia due to impaired cells that line the lungs.

Decreased vitamin A levels that do not necessarily cause outward symptoms can nonetheless lead to childhood issues such as increased infections, decreased growth and slow bone development, as well as increased chance of death from serious illness.[11,12] One important thing to note about vitamin A deficiency is that outside of inadequate dietary intake, excessive alcohol consumption can deplete vitamin A levels.

Where to find them: Livers, sweet potatoes, carrots (carotenoids, anyone?), butter, spinach, pumpkin, cheddar cheese, eggs, apricots, mangoes, peas, cantaloupe, peppers, broccoli.

B Vitamins

There are a decent amount of different B vitamins around the street, so for our run through here we can focus on three specific ones - B12 (cobalamin), B9 (folate), and B6 (pyridoxine). Of those three, B9 is the one that is practically never referred to as B9 but rather as folate or more commonly known as folic acid. Let's take a tour of some benefits associated with the vitamins and dangers of deficiency.

Vitamin B12 is a bit of a hard hitter and has functions in the formation of red blood cells, proper neural function, and the creation of DNA.[13-17] Vitamin B6 is a part of a large amount of enzymatic reactions, aids in the creation of neurotransmitters, functions in sugar creation, and has its fingers in the immune system pie.[17,18] Folate has a large role in decreasing birth defects, as it is very important for the production and maintenance of new cells, as well as being required to make both RNA and DNA.[19]

Deficiencies of vitamin B12 can range from numbness of feet to confusion, dementia, depression, and our personal favorite - a sore tongue.[20] Vitamin B6 deficiency can lead to irritability and seizures in infants, and for everyone in general decreased immune function and depression.[17,21] Other than the aforementioned birth defects, low levels of folate seem to be associated with increased risks of cancers such as breast, pancreatic, and colon cancers.[22-24]

Where to find them:
B12 - Clams, liver, trout, salmon, tuna, beef, cheese, yogurt, milk, ham, eggs.
B9 - Beef liver, lentils, spinach, egg noodles, asparagus, macaroni, rice.
B6 - Chickpeas, beef liver, tuna, salmon, chicken breast, potatoes, turkey, bananas, squash, cottage cheese.

Vitamin C

While many animals are able to create vitamin C within their own bodies, humans drew the short straw there and cannot. We would say we made this up by eating said animals, but fruits and vegetables are overwhelmingly the providers of vitamin C. This vitamin is the most popular supplement consumed, no doubt due to societal flashbacks of pirate incursions and wishing for that never to return.

The more well-known association that vitamin C has is with the immune system, and this is indeed part of its functionality, as well as its activity as a potent antioxidant.[25,26] It can even help restore amounts of other antioxidants such as vitamin E. On the construction side, vitamin C helps with the assembly of neurotransmitters and collagen, as well as being a factor in the metabolic activity of proteins.[27,28] Vitamin C is also an important antihistamine, with noted benefits of supplementation and increased histamine levels due to deficiency.[29-31] Antihistamines are well known for reducing or preventing allergic reactions.

It goes without saying that we will once again mention scurvy as a result of vitamin C deficiency.[32-34] After all, weakness, swollen gums, loose teeth, inadequate wound healing, joint pain, and a host of other issues are no walk in the park. Oh, and scurvy being fatal if untreated isn't so hot either.[35,36]

Where to find it: Peppers, oranges, grapefruits, kiwi, lemons, tomatoes, broccoli, cabbage, potatoes, strawberries, Brussels sprouts.

Where not to find it: 17th century pirate ships.

Vitamin E

Vitamin E and vitamin C are often taken together. While vitamin C dissolves in water, vitamin E dissolves in fat. While there are many forms of vitamin E, as far as supplements go the most appropriate way to go about taking one is a combination of gamma, alpha, beta, and delta isomers, and not just one variant.

Vitamin E is of course a potent antioxidant, a function many are aware of.[37] Through specific enzymatic action, vitamin E can reduce the tendency of platelets to cluster together which if done at inopportune times can lead to a blood clot, the kind inside the blood vessel that you definitely don't want to get.[33] Vitamin E is a factor in various functions such as metabolic processes, immune function, and the expression of genes.[38]

The primary association with a deficiency of Vitamin E relates to poor neural function. Malfunctions associated with this deficiency can include a lack of coordinated voluntary movement, muscular weakness, and nerve damage.[39-46] Vitamin E deficiency is also related to decreased red blood cell life span.[47,48] Fortunately for all involved, vitamin E deficiency is relatively rare.

Where to find it: Sunflower seeds, almonds, peanuts, hazelnuts, corn oil, olive oil.

Vitamin D

Ah yes, "Vitamin D." An essential vitamin that should be a part of the diet, just waiting to be absorbed. We have dismissed that claim. It is certainly very important, playing roles in bone growth and restructuring, preventing rickets in children, and functioning in cell growth, immune function, and reducing inflammation.[49-52] However, it shouldn't particularly be called a vitamin. Base definition of a vitamin is a nutrient, meaning something essential for the body to have that is taken in from the environment. Vitamin D is actually a secosteroid that is found in few foods naturally (but is added as a fortifying agent when appropriate to combat deficiency).

Vitamin D is produced in our bodies when the sun hits our skin. Therefore, while we can certainly get scant vitamin D from our foods naturally (or in large part due to the food producers putting it in), the majority of production is within our own body, which somewhat takes away vitamin D's place at the vitamin table. The reason for it being called a vitamin is because the discovery happened early in the 20th century, when scientists were on a roll of new understanding. Vitamin D just happened to be discovered around the time other vitamins were, so it got slapped with this wrong label. We simply added vitamin D here because it is considered part of the "major vitamins" and did not want to provide undue confusion by its absence.

Where to find it: Go outside. Barring that, fish such as tuna and salmon, and the many dairy products that are fortified with vitamin D.

As we stated from the beginning, this is not meant to be an all-inclusive list of every action and benefit of all the nutrients that we get from food. This is simply an example of why the "healthy" food is healthy. Such an endeavor would fill an encyclopedia. Further information is readily available with raw scientific data from reputable sources for you to peruse on the internet.

Epilogue

Thus ends our journey through a variant of medicine that is quickly growing in popularity as people find out - hey, this makes sense. We hope that you were both equally educated and entertained. There is a lot of information out there about the physiologic approach and its applications, and it's only necessary to put the information together to make an informed decision and to utilize it. Remember, the information is out there for you to look through. Use the knowledge you gain to stay healthy and most of all make sure that you get plenty of vitamin C so that you don't turn into a pirate.

Thanks for reading. Remember, knowledge is power - go out and get it.

References

Part I

1. Krabbendam L, van Os J. Schizophrenia and urbanicity: a major environmental influence—conditional on genetic risk. Schizophr Bull. 2005;31:795–9.

2. Cantor-Graae E, Selten JP. Schizophrenia and migration: a meta-analysis and review. Am J Psychiatry. 2005;162:12–24.

3. Boydell J, Van Os J, McKenzie K, Allardyce J, Goel R, McCreadie RG, Murray RM. Incidence of schizophrenia in ethnic minorities in London: ecological study into interactions with environment. BMJ. 2001;323:1336.

4. Veling W, Susser E, van Os J, Mackenbach JP, Selten JP, Hoek HW. Ethnic density of neighborhoods and incidence of psychotic disorders among immigrants. Am J Psychiatry. 2008;165:66–73.

5. Moore TH, Zammit S, Lingford-Hughes A, Barnes TR, Jones PB, Burke M, Lewis G. Cannabis use and risk of psychotic or affective mental health outcomes: a systematic review. Lancet. 2007;370:319–28.

6. D'Souza DC, Abi-Saab WM, Madonick S, Forcelius-Bielen K, Doersch A, Braley G, et al. Delta-9-tetra hydrocannabinol effects in schizophrenia: implications for cognition, psychosis, and addiction. Biol Psychiatry. 2005;57:594–608.

7. Henquet C, Rosa A, Krabbendam L, Papiol S, Fananas L, Drukker M, et al. An experimental study of catechol-o-methyltransferase Val158Met moderation of delta-9-tetrahydrocannabinol-induced effects on psychosis and cognition. Neuropsychopharmacology. 2006;31:2748–57.

8. Smith CA, Harrison DJ. Association between polymorphism in gene for microsomal epoxide hydrolase and susceptibility to emphysema. Lancet. 1997;350:630–3.

9. Herder C, Roden M. Genetics of type 2 diabetes: pathophysiologic and clinical relevance. Eur J Clin Invest. 2011;41(6):679-92.

10. Kapil U. Successful efforts toward elimination iodine deficiency in India. Indian J Community Med. 2010;35(4):455-68.

Part II

1. Feldmann H, Geisbert TW. Ebola haemorrhagic fever. Lancet. 2011;377(9768):849-62.

2. Mayne L, Girod C, Weltz S. 2011 Millman Medical Index. May 2012. Available at: http://publications.milliman.com/periodicals/mmi/pdfs/milliman-medical-index-2011.pdf. Accessed April 3, 2012.

3. Starfield B. Is US health really the best in the world? JAMA. 2000;284(4):483-5.

4. Smith D. Cardiovascular disease: a historic perspective. Jpn J Vet Res. 2000;48(2-3):147-66.

5. Jacobson TA. Clinical context: current concepts of coronary heart disease management. Am J Med. 2001;110 Suppl 6A:3S-11S.

6. Held C, Iqbal R, Lear SA, Rosengren A, Islam S, Matthew J, Yusuf S. Physical activity levels, ownership of goods promoting sedentary behaviour and risk of myocardial infarction: results of the INTERHEART study. Eur Heart J. 2012 Feb;33(4):452-66.

7. Yusuf S, Hawken S, Ounpuu S, Dans T, Avezum A, Lanas F, et al. Effect of potentially modifiable risk factors associated with myocardial infarction in 52 countries (the INTERHEART study): case-control study. Lancet. 2004 Sep 11-17;364(9438):937-52.

8. Barness LA, Opitz JM, Gilbert-Barness E. Obesity: genetic, molecular, and environmental aspects. Am J Med Genet A. 2007;143A(24):3016–34.

9. Rocchini AP. Obesity hypertension. Am J Hypertens. 2002;15(2 Pt 2):50S-2S.

10. Haslam DW, James WP. Obesity. Lancet. 2005;366(9492):1197-209.

11. Mariolis P, Rock VJ, Asman K, Merritt R, Malarcher A, Husten C, et al. Tobacco Use Among Adults --- United States, 2005. Available at: http://www.cdc.gov/mmwr/preview/mmwrhtml/mm5542a1.htm. Accessed April 3, 2012.

12. U.S. Obesity Trends. Available at: http://www.cdc.gov/obesity/data/trends.html. Accessed April 5, 2012.

13. Velazquez EJ, Lee KL, Deja MA, Jain A, Sopko G, Marchenko A, et al. Coronary-artery bypass surgery in patients with left ventricular dysfunction. N Engl J Med. 2011 Apr 28;364(17):1607–16.

14. Weintraub WS, Spertus JA, Kolm P, Maron DJ, Zhang Z, Jurkovitz C, et al. Effect of PCI on quality of life in patients with stable coronary artery disease. N Engl J Med. 2008 Aug 14;359(7):677-87.

15. Boden WE, O'Rourke RA, Teo KK, Hartigan PM, Maron DJ, Kostuk WJ, et al. Optimal medical therapy with or without PCI for stable coronary disease. N Engl J Med. 2007 Apr 12;356(15):1503-16.

16. Ornish D. Integrative Care: A Pathway to a Healthier Nation. Available at: http://www.help.senate.gov/imo/media/doc/Ornish.pdf. Accessed April 6, 2012.

17. Adams KM, Lindell KC, Kohlmeier M, Zeisel SH. Status of nutrition education in medical schools. Am J Clin Nutr. 2006;83(4):941S-4S.

18. Silver MA, Langsjoen PH, Szabo S, Patil H, Zelinger A. Statin cardiomyopathy? A potential role for Co-Enzyme Q10 therapy for statin-induced changes in diastolic LV performance: description of a clinical protocol. Biofactors. 2003;18(1-4):125-7.

19. Sauret JM, Marinides G, Wang GK. Rhabdomyolysis. Am Fam Physician. 2002;65(5):907–12.

20. Zeitlinger M, Müller M. [Clinico-pharmacologic explanation models of cerivastatin associated rhabdomyolysis]. Wien Med Wochenschr. 2003;153(11–12):250–4.

21. Muldoon MF, Ryan CM, Flory JD, Manuck SB. Effects of simvastatin on cognitive functioning. Presented at the American Heart Association Scientific Sessions. Chicago, IL, USA. 2002, Nov. 17-20.

22. Wagstaff LR, Mitton MW, Arvik BM, Doraiswamy PM. Statin-associated memory loss: analysis of 60 case reports and review of the literature. Pharmacotherapy. 2003 Jul;23(7):871-80.

23. King DS, Wilburn AJ, Wofford MR, Harrell TK, Lindley BJ, Jones DW. Cognitive impairment associated with atorvastatin and simvastatin. Pharmacotherapy. 2003 Dec;23(12):1663-7.

24. Orsi A, Sherman O, Woldeselassie Z. Simvastatin-associated memory loss. Pharmacotherapy. 2001 Jun;21(6):767-9.

25. Gaist D, García Rodríguez LA, Huerta C, Hallas J, Sindrup SH. Are users of lipid-lowering drugs at increased risk of peripheral neuropathy? Eur J Clin Pharmacol. 2001 Mar;56(12):931-3.

26. Ahmad A, Fletcher MT, Roy TM. Simvastatin-induced lupus-like syndrome. Tenn Med. 2000 Jan;93(1):21-2.

27. McPherson R, Hanna K, Agro A, Braeken A; Canadian Cerivastatin Study Group. Cerivastatin versus branded pravastatin in the treatment of primary hypercholesterolemia in primary care practice in Canada: a one-year, open-label, randomized, comparative study of efficacy, safety, and cost-effectiveness. Clin Ther. 2001 Sep;23(9):1492-507.

28. Smith GD, Song F, Sheldon TA. Cholesterol lowering and mortality: the importance of considering initial level of risk. BMJ. 1993 May 22;306(6889):1367-73.

29. Childs M, Girardot G. Evaluation of acquired data on long-term risk of hypolipidemic treatments. Arch Mal Coeur Vaiss. 1992 Sep;85 Spec No 2:129-33.

30. Banga JD. Myotoxicity and rhabdomyolisis due to statins. Ned Tijdschr Geneeskd. 2001;145(49):2371-6.

31. Simons LA, Levis G, Simons J. Apparent discontinuation rates in patients prescribed lipid-lowering drugs. Med J Aust. 1996 Feb 19;164(4):208-11.

32. Zhang D, Sun Y, Yue Z, Li Q, Meng J, Liu J, et al. Apple polysaccharides induce apoptosis in colorectal cancer cells. Int J Mol Med. 2012 Jul;30(1):100-6.

33. Available at: http://news.harvard.edu/gazette/story/2009/09/new-study-finds-45000-deaths-annually-linked-to-lack-of-health-coverage/. Accessed April 6, 2012.

Part III

1. Guerin JC. Emerging area of aging research: long-lived animals with "negligible senescence". Ann N Y Acad Sci. 2004 Jun;1019:518-20.

2. Salimpoor VN, Benovoy M, Larcher K, Dagher A, Zatorre RJ. Anatomically distinct dopamine release during anticipation and experience of peak emotion to music. Nat Neurosci. 2011; 14(2):257-62.

3. Hof PR, Mobbs CV. Handbook of the neuroscience of aging. London: Elsevier. 2009. ISBN 9780123748980.

4. Paul SM, Purdy RH. Neuroactive steroids. FASEB J. 1992 Mar;6(6):2311-22.

5. Azevedo F, Carvalho L, Grinberg L, Farfel J, Ferretti R, Leite, R, et al. Equal numbers of neuronal and nonneuronal cells make the human brain an isometrically scaled-up primate brain. J Comp Neurol. 2009 Apr 10;513(5):532-41.

6. Roberts E, Fitten LJ. Serum steroid levels in two old men with Alzheimer's disease (AD) before and after oral administration of dehydroepiandrosterone (DHEA). Pregnenolone synthesis may be ratelimiting in aging. In: Kalimi M, Regelson W, editors. The Biological Role of Dehydroepiandrosterone (DHEA). Berlin , de Gruyter, 1990;43–63.

7. Semeniuk T, Jhangri GS, Le Mellédo JM. Neuroactive steroid levels in patients with generalized anxiety disorder. J Neuropsychiatry Clin Neurosci. 2001 Summer;13(3):396-8.

8. Ballenger, JC; Davidson, JR, Lecrubier, Y, Nutt, DJ, Borkovec, TD, Rickels, K, et al. Consensus statement on generalized anxiety disorder from the International Consensus Group on Depression and Anxiety. J Clin Psychiatry. 2001;62 Suppl 11:53-8.

9. George MS, Guidotti A, Rubinow D, Pan B, Mikalauskas K, Post RM. CSF neuroactive steroids in affective disorders: pregnenolone, progesterone, and DBI. Biol Psychiatry. 1994 May 15;35(10):775-80.

10. Osuji IJ, Vera-Bolaños E, Carmody TJ, Brown ES. Pregnenolone for cognition and mood in dual diagnosis patients. Psychiatry Res. 2010 Jul 30;178(2):309-12.

11. Roberts E. Pregneolone—from Selye to Alzheimer and a model of the pregnenolone sulfate binding site on the GABAA receptor. Biochem Pharmacol. 1995 Jan 6;49(1):1-16.

12. Copeland JL, Consitt LA, Tremblay MS. Hormonal responses to endurance and resistance exercise in females aged 19-69 years. J Gerontol A Biol Sci Med Sci. 2002 Apr;57(4):B158-65.

13. Ganong WF. Review of Medical Physiology. 22nd Ed, McGraw Hill. 2005; 362.

14. The Merck Index, 13th Edition, 7798.

15. Schulman RA, Dean Carolyn. DHEA (Dehydroepiandrosterone) is a common hormone produced in the adrenal glands, the gonads, and the brain. In: Solve it with supplements. New York City: Rodale, Inc. 2007;100. ISBN 978-1-57954-942-8.

16. Dharia S, Parker CR Jr. Adrenal androgens and aging. Semin Reprod Med. 2004 Nov;22(4):361-8.

17. Bélanger A, Candas B, Dupont A, Cusan L, Diamond P, Gomez JL, et al. Changes in serum concentrations of conjugated and unconjugated steroids in 40- to 80-year-old men. J Clin Endocrinol Metab. 1994 Oct;79(4):1086-90.

18. Labrie F, Bélanger A, Cusan L, Gomez JL, Candas B. Marked decline in serum concentrations of adrenal C19 sex steroid precursors and conjugated androgen metabolites during aging. J Clin Endocrinol Metab. 1997 Aug;82(8):2396-402.

19. Barad D, Brill H, Gleicher N. Update on the use of dehydroepiandrosterone supplementation among women with diminished ovarian function. J Assist Reprod Genet. 2007 Dec;24(12):629-34.

20. Casson PR, Lindsay MS, Pisarska MD, Carson SA, Buster JE. Dehydroepiandrosterone supplementation augments ovarian stimulation in poor responders: a case series. Hum Reprod. 2000;15:2129-32.

21. Barrett-Connor E, Khaw KT Yen SS. A prospective study of dehydroepiandrosterone sulfate, mortality, and cardiovascular disease. N Eng J Med. 1986 Dec;315:1519-24.

22. Alhaj HA, Massey AE, McAllister-Williams RH. Effects of DHEA administration on episodic memory, cortisol and mood in healthy young men: a double-blind, placebo-controlled study. Psychopharmacology (Berl). 2006 Nov;188(4):541-51.

23. Bloch M, Schmidt PJ, Danaceau MA, Adams LF, Rubinow DR. Dehydroepiandrosterone treatment of midlife dysthymia. Biol Psychiatry. 1999 Jun 15;45(12):1533-41.

24. Wolkowitz OM, Reus VI, Roberts E, Manfredi F, Chan T, Raum WJ, et al. Dehydroepiandrosterone (DHEA) treatment of depression. Biol Psychiatry. 1997 Feb 1;41(3):311-8.

25. Salom MG, Jabaloyas JM. [Testosterone deficit syndrome and erectile dysfunction]. Arch Esp Urol. 2010 Oct;63(8):663-70.

26. Panay N, Al-Azzawi F, Bouchard C, Davis SR, Eden J, Lodhi I, et al. Testosterone treatment of HSDD in naturally menopausal women: the ADORE study. Climacteric. 2010 Apr;13(2):121-31.

27. Malkin CJ, Pugh PJ, Morris PD, Asif S, Jones TH, Channer KS. Low serum testosterone and increased mortality in men with coronary heart disease. Heart. 2010 Nov;96(22):1821-5.

28. Iellamo F, Volterrani M, Caminiti G, Karam R, Massaro R, Fini M, et al. Testosterone therapy in women with chronic heart failure: a pilot double-blind, randomized, placebo-controlled study. J Am Coll Cardiol. 2010 Oct 12;56(16):1310-6.

29. Białek M, Zaremba P, Borowicz KK, Czuczwar SJ. Neuroprotective role of testosterone in the nervous system. Pol J Pharmacol. 2004 Sep-Oct;56(5):509-18.

30. Pentikäinen V, Erkkilä K, Suomalainen L, Parvinen M, Dunkel L. Estradiol acts as a germ cell survival factor in the human testis in vitro. J Clin Endocrinol Metab. 2000 May;85(5):2057-67.

31. Craig MC, Murphy DG. Estrogen therapy and Alzheimer's dementia. Ann N Y Acad Sci. 2010 Sep;1205:245-53.

32. Douma SL, Husband C, O'Donnell ME, Barwin BN, Woodend AK. Estrogen-related mood disorders: reproductive life cycle factors. ANS Adv Nurs Sci. 2005 Oct-Dec;28(4):364-75.

33. Sánchez MG, Bourque M, Morissette M, Di Paolo T. Steroids-dopamine interactions in the pathophysiology and treatment of CNS disorders. CNS Neurosci Ther. 2010 Jun;16(3):e43-71.

34. Hu Z, Li Y, Fang M, Wai MS, Yew DT. Exogenous progesterone: a potential therapeutic candidate in CNS injury and neurodegeneration. Curr Med Chem. 2009;16(11):1418-25.

35. Oettel M, Mukhopadhyay AK. Progesterone: the forgotten hormone in men? Aging Male. 2004 Sep;7(3):236-57.

Part IV

1. Fournier A, Berrino F, Clavel-Chapelon F. Unequal risks for breast cancer associated with different hormone replacement therapies: results from the E3N cohort study. Breast Cancer Res Treat. 2008 Jan;107(1):103-11.

2. Rossouw JE, Anderson GL, Prentice RL, LaCroix AZ, Kooperberg C, Stefanick ML, et al. Risks and benefits of estrogen plus progestin in healthy postmenopausal women: principal results From the Women's Health Initiative randomized controlled trial. JAMA. 2002 Jul 17;288(3):321-33.

3. Ziel HK, Finkle WD. Increased risk of endometrial carcinoma among users of conjugated estrogens. N Engl J Med. 1975 Dec 4;293(23):1167-70.

4. Garcia-Santos G, Martin V, Rodriguez-Blanco J, Herrera F, Casado-Zapico S, Sanchez-Sanchez AM, et al. Fas/Fas ligand regulation mediates cell death in human Ewing's sarcoma cells treated with melatonin. Br J Cancer. 2012;106(7):1288-96.

5. Available at:
    http://www.nlm.nih.gov/medlineplus/ency/article/002423.htm.
    Accessed April 12, 2012.

6. Rude RK, Shils ME. Magnesium. In: Shils ME, Shike M, Ross AC,
    Caballero B, Cousins RJ, eds. Modern Nutrition in Health and Disease.
    10th ed. Baltimore: Lippincott Williams & Wilkins. 2006;223-247.

7. Blaylock RL. Health and Nutrition Secrets. Health Pres. 2006;395.
    ISBN 978-0-929173-48-1.

8. Available   at:
    http://www.ars.usda.gov/Services/docs.htm?docid=15677.   Accessed
    April 12, 2012.

9. Available at: http://ehealthmd.com/content/what-causes-prostate-
    enlarge. Accessed April 13, 2012.

10. Berdanier CD, Dwyer JT, Feldman EB. Handbook of Nutrition and
    Food. Boca Raton, Florida: CRC Press. 2007.
    ISBN 0-8493-9218-7.

11. Age-Related Eye Disease Study Research Group. A randomized,
    placebo-controlled, clinical trial of high-dose supplementation with
    vitamins C and E, beta carotene, and zinc for age-related macular
    degeneration and vision loss: AREDS report no. 8. Arch Ophthalmol.
    2001 Oct;119(10):1417–36.

Part V

1. Available at:
   http://www.sigmaaldrich.com/Area_of_Interest/Biochemicals/Enzyme_Explorer/Key_Resources/Plasma__Blood_Protein/Lipoprotein_Function.html Accessed April 29, 2012.

2. Martin U, Davies C, Hayavi S, Hartland A, Dunne F. Is normal pregnancy atherogenic? Clin Sci (Lond). 1999 Apr;96(4):421-5.

3. Warth MR, Arky RA, Knopp RH. Lipid metabolism in pregnancy. II. Altered lipid composition in intermediage, very low, low and high-density lipoprotein fractions. J Clin Endocrinol Metab. 1975 Oct;41(4):649-55.

4. Sitadevi C, Patrudu MB, Kumar YM, Raju GR, Suryaprabha K. Longitudinal study of serum lipids and lipoproteins in normal pregnancy and puerperium. Trop Geogr Med. 1981 Sep;33(3):219-23.

5. Brizzi P, Tonolo G, Esposito F, Puddu L, Dessole S, Maioli M, et al. Lipoprotein metabolism during normal pregnancy. Am J Obstet Gynecol. 1999 Aug;181(2):430-4.

6. Troisi A, Moles A, Panepuccia L, Lo Russo D, Palla G, Scucchi S. Serum cholesterol levels and mood symptoms in the postpartum period. Psychiatry Res. 2002 Apr 15;109(3):213-9.

7. Mizuno O, Yokoyama T, Tsutsumi N. The changes of serum total cholesterol, HDL-cholesterol and atherogenic index in postpartum. Nippon Sanka Fujinka Gakkai Zasshi. 1984 Dec;36(12):2593-7.

8. Erkkola R, Viikari J, Irjala K, Solakivi-Jaakkola T. One-year follow-up of lipoprotein metabolism after pregnancy. Biol Res Pregnancy Perinatol. 1986;7(2):47-51.

9. Smolarczyk R, Romejko E, Wójcicka-Jagodzińska J, Czajkowski K, Teliga-Czajkowska J, Piekarski P. Lipid metabolism in women with threatened abortion. Ginekol Pol. 1996 Oct;67(10):481-7.

10. Samánek M, Urbanová Z. Cholesterol and triglyceride levels and their development from 2 to 17 years of age. Cas Lek Cesk. 1997 Jun 12;136(12):380-5.

11. Rodkiewicz B, Szotowa W, Woynarowska B, Cerańska-Goszczyńska H, Ignar-Golinowska B, Pułtorak M.. Serum cholesterol levels in children aged 4-14 years. Probl Med Wieku Rozwoj. 1984;13:95-102.

12. Lin CC, Lai MM, Liu CS, Li TC. Serum cholesterol levels and prevalence of hypercholesterolemia in school-aged Taiwanese children and adolescents: the Taichung Study. Zhonghua Yi Xue Za Zhi (Taipei). 1999 Nov;62(11):787-94.

13. Lerman-Garber I, Sepúlveda-Amor JA, Tapia-Conyer R, Magos-López C, Cardoso-Saldaña G, Zamora-González J, et al. Cholesterol levels and prevalence of hypercholesterolemia in Mexican children and teenagers. Atherosclerosis. 1993 Nov;103(2):195-203.

14. Suthutvoravut U, Charoenkiatkul S, Chitchumroonchokchai C, Kosulwat V, Mahachoklertwattana P, Rojroongwasinkul N. Elevated serum cholesterol levels in Bangkok children and adolescents. J Med Assoc Thai. 1999 Nov;82 Suppl 1:S117-21.

15. Lehtonen A, Viikari J. Serum lipids in soccer and ice-hockey players. Metabolism. 1980 Jan;29(1):36-9.

16. Boston PF, Dursun SM, Reveley MA. Cholesterol and mental disorder. Br J Psychiatry. 1996 Dec;169(6):682-9.

17. Bostom AG, Cupples LA, Jenner JL, Ordovas JM, Seman LJ, Wilson PW, et al. Lipoprotein(a)-cholesterol and coronary heart disease in the Framingham Heart Study. Clin Chem. 1999;45(7):1039-46.

18. Papassotiropoulos A, Hawellek B, Frahnert C, Rao GS, Rao ML. The risk of acute suicidality in psychiatric inpatients increases with low plasma cholesterol. Pharmacopsychiatry. 1999;32(1):1-4.

19. Gould AL, Rossouw JE, Santanello NC, Heyse JF, Furberg CD. Cholesterol reduction yields clinical benefit. A new look at old data. Circulation. 1995;91(8):2274-82.

20. Jakovljević M, Reiner Z, Milicić D. Mental disorders, treatment response, mortality and serum cholesterol: a new holistic look at old data. Psychiatr Danub. 2007 Dec;19(4):270-81.

21. Windler E, Ewers-Grabow U, Thiery J, Walli A, Seidel D, Greten H. The prognostic value of hypocholesterolemia in hospitalized patients. Clin Investig. 1994 Dec;72(12):939-43.

22. Onder G, Landi F, Volpato S, Fellin R, Carbonin P, Gambassi G, et al. Serum cholesterol levels and in-hospital mortality in the elderly. Am J Med. 2003 Sep;115(4):265-71.

23. Corti MC, Guralnik JM, Salive ME, Harris T, Ferrucci L, Glynn RJ, et al. Clarifying the direct relation between total cholesterol levels and death from coronary heart disease in older persons. Ann Intern Med. 1997 May 15;126(10):753-60.

24. Krumholz HM, Seeman TE, Merrill SS, Mendes de Leon CF, Vaccarino V, Silverman DI, et al. Lack of association between cholesterol and coronary heart disease mortality and morbidity and all-cause mortality in persons older than 70 years. JAMA. 1994 Nov 2;272(17):1335-40.

25. Stemmermann GN, Chyou PH, Kagan A, Nomura AM, Yano K. Serum cholesterol and mortality among Japanese-American men. The Honolulu (Hawaii) Heart Program. Arch Intern Med. 1991 May;151(5):969-72.

26. Navab M, Van Lenten BJ, Reddy ST, Fogelman AM. High-density lipoprotein and the dynamics of atherosclerotic lesions. Circulation. 2001 Nov 13;104(20):2386-7.

27. Siemianowicz K, Gminski J, Stajszczyk M, Wojakowski W, Goss M, Machalski M, et al. Serum total cholesterol and triglycerides levels in patients with lung cancer. Int J Mol Med. 2000 Feb;5(2):201-5.

28. Williams RR, Sorlie PD, Feinleib M, McNamara PM, Kannel WB, Dawber TR. Cancer incidence by levels of cholesterol. JAMA. 1981 Jan 16;245(3):247-52.

29. Törnberg SA, Carstensen JM, Holm LE. Risk of stomach cancer in association with serum cholesterol and beta-lipoprotein. Acta Oncol. 1988;27(1):39-42.

30. Knekt P, Reunanen A, Aromaa A, Heliövaara M, Hakulinen T, Hakama M. Serum cholesterol and risk of cancer in a cohort of 39,000 men and women. Clin Epidemiol. 1988;41(6):519-30.

31. Goldstein MR, Mascitelli L. Do statins decrease cardiovascular disease at the expense of increasing cancer? Int J Cardiol. 2009 Apr 3;133(2):254-5.

32. Iribarren C, Jacobs DR Jr, Sidney S, Claxton AJ, Gross MD, Sadler M, et al. Serum total cholesterol and risk of hospitalization, and death from respiratory disease. Int J Epidemiol. 1997 Dec;26(6):1191-202.

33. Fraunberger P, Schaefer S, Werdan K, Walli AK, Seidel D. Reduction of circulating cholesterol and apolipoprotein levels during sepsis. Clin Chem Lab Med. 1999 Mar;37(3):357-62.

34. Claxton AJ, Jacobs DR Jr, Iribarren C, Welles SL, Sidney S, Feingold KR. Association between serum total cholesterol and HIV infection in a high-risk cohort of young men. J Acquir Immune Defic Syndr Hum Retrovirol. 1998 Jan 1;17(1):51-7.

35. Shor-Posner G, Basit A, Lu Y, Cabrejos C, Chang J, Fletcher M, et al. Hypocholesterolemia is associated with immune dysfunction in early human immunodeficiency virus-1 infection. Am J Med. 1993 May;94(5):515-9.

36. Leardi S, Altilia F, Delmonaco S, Cianca G, Pietroletti R, Simi M. Blood levels of cholesterol and postoperative septic complications. Ann Ital Chir. 2000 Mar-Apr;71(2):233-7.

37. Ormiston T, Wolkowitz OM, Reus VI, Johnson R, Manfredi F. Hormonal changes with cholesterol reduction: a double-blind pilot study. J Clin Pharm Ther. 2004 Feb;29(1):71-3.

38. Dzugan SA, Rozakis GW, Dzugan SS, Smith RA. Hormonorestorative therapy is a promising method for hypercholesterolemia treatment. Approaches to Aging Control. 2009;13:12-9.

39. Dzugan SA, Rozakis GW, Dzugan KS, Emhof L, Dzugan SS, Xydas C, et al. Correction of Steroidopenia as a New Method of Hypercholesterolemia Treatment. Neuroendocrinol Lett (NEL). 2011;32(1):77-81.

40. Smith D. Cardiovascular disease: a historic perspective. Jpn J Vet Res. 2000 Nov;48(2-3):147-66.

41. Jacobson TA. Clinical context: current concepts of coronary heart disease management. Am J Med. 2001 Apr 16;110 Suppl 6A:3S-11S.

42. Weiner SD, Reis ED, Kerstein MD. Peripheral arterial disease. Medical management in primary care practice. Geriartrics. 2001 Apr;56(4):20-2, 25-6, 29-30.

43. Soska V. Pharmacotherapy of hyperlipoproteinemia. Vnitr Lek. 2000 Sep;46(9):565-8.

44. Hanefeld M, Hora C, Schulze J, Rothe G, Barthel U, Haller H. Reduced incidence of cardiovascular complications and mortality in hyperlipoproteinemia (HLP) with effective lipid correction. The Dresden HLP study. Atherosclerosis. 1984 Oct;53(1):47-58.

45. Vogel RA, Corretti MC, Gellman J. Cholesterol, cholesterol lowering, and endothelial function. Prog Cardiovasc Dis. 1998 Sep-Oct;41(2):117-36

46. Lopez-Sendon JL, Rubio R, Lopez de Sa E, Delcan JL. Why the cardiologists should be interested in lipids? Rev Esp Cardiol. 1995;48 Suppl 2:23-32.

47. Hughes K. Screening for and treatment of hypercholesterolemia – a review. Ann Acad Med Singapore. 1997 Mar;26(2):215-20.

48. Yang YH, Kao SM, Chan KW. A retrospective drug utilization of antihyperlipidaemic agents in a medical center in Taiwan. J Clin Pharm Ther. 1997 Aug;22(4):291-9.

49. Turpin G, Bruckert E. Management of atherogenic hyperlipidemia. Ann Cardiol Angeiol (Paris). 1998 Nov;47(9):627-32.

50. Bancarz A, Jolda-Mydlovska B, Swidnicka-Szuszkowska B. [Pharmacological treatment of lipid disorders according to present clinical studies]. Pol Merkur Lekarski. 1998 Sep;5(27):162-6.

51. Bachmann GA. Androgen cotherapy in menopause: evolving benefits and challenges. Am J Obstet Gynecol. 1999 Mar;180(3 Pt 2):S308-11.

52. Ciepluch R, Czestochowska E. Hormonal replacement therapy and body weight in postmenopausal women. Pol Merkur Lekarski. 1997 Jan;2(9):188-90.

53. Regelson W, Loria R, Kalimi M. Hormonal intervention: "buffer hormones" or "state dependency". The role of dehydroepiandrosterone (DHEA), thyroid hormone, estrogen and hypophysectomy in aging. Ann NY Acad Sci. 1988;521:260-73.

54. Morales AJ, Nolan JJ, Nelson JC, Yen SS. Effects of replacement dose of dehydroepiandrosterone in men and women of advancing age. J Clin Endocrinol Metab. 1994. Jun;78(6):1360-7.

55. Takahashi K, Manabe A, Okada M, Kurioka H, Kanasaki H, Miyazaki K. Efficacy and safety of oral estriol for managing postmenopausal symptoms. Maturitas. 2000 Feb 15;34(2):169-77.

56. Haddock BL, Marshak HP, Mason JJ, Blix G. The effect of hormone replacement therapy and exercise on cardiovascular disease risk factors in postmenopausal women. Sports Med. 2000. Jan;29(1):39-49.

57. Kummerow FA, Olinescu RM, Fleischer L, Handler B, Shinkareva SV. The relationship of oxidized lipids to coronary artery stenosis. Atherosclerosis. 2000;149:181-190.

58. Bratus' VV, Talaieva TV, Lomakovs'kyĭ OM, Tretiak IV, Radalovs'ka NV. Modified lipoproteins – their types and role in atherogenesis. Fiziol Zh. 2000;46:73-81.

59. Haug A, Hostmark AT, Spydevold O. Plasma lipoprotein responses to castration and androgen substitution in rats. Metabolism. 1984;33:465-470.

60. Hänggi W, Birkhäuser MH, Malek A, Peheim E, von Hospenthal JU. Cyclical gestagen (MPA) supplement for continuous transdermal or oral estrogen substitution in postmenopause: modification of serum lipids. Geburtshilfe Frauenheilkd. 1993;53:709-14.

61. Dzugan SA, Smith RA. Broad spectrum restoration in natural steroid hormones as possible treatment for hypercholesterolemia. Bull Urg Rec Med. 2002;3: 278-84.

62. Dzugan SA, Smith RA. Hypercholesterolemia treatment: a new hypothesis or just an accident? Med Hypotheses. 2002;59:751-6.

63. Dzugan SA. Hypercholesterolemia treatment: a new hypothesis or just an accident. In: Anti-Aging Therapeutics. Vol. 6. Chicago, IL, USA. 2004;89-98.

64. Dzugan SA, Smith RA, Kuznetsov AS. A new statin free method of hypercholesterolemia. Health Donbass. 2004;4:19-25.

65. Dzugan SA. Hypercholesterolemia Treatment: a New Statin Free Method. In: Anti-Aging Therapeutics. Vol. 9. Chicago, IL, USA. 2007;117-25.

66. Dzugan SA, Rozakis GW, Dzugan SS, Smith RA. Hormonorestorative therapy is a promising method for hypercholesterolemia treatment. Approaches to Aging Control. 2009;13:12-9.

Part VI

1. Krippendorf, BB; Riley, DA. Distinguishing unloading-versus reloading-induced changes in rat soleus muscle. Muscle Nerve. 1993;16(1):99–108.

2. St Pierre BA, Tidball JG. Differential response of macrophage subpopulations to soleus muscle reloading following rat hindlimb suspension. J Appl Physiol. 1994 Jul;77(1):290-7.

3. Tidball JG, Berchenko E, Frenette J. Macrophage invasion does not contribute to muscle membrane injury during inflammation. J Leukoc Biol. 1999 Apr;65(4):492-8.

4. Brechot N, Gomez E, Bignon M, Khallou-Laschet J, Dussiot M, Cazes A, et al. Modulation of Macrophage Activation State Protects Tissue from Necrosis during Critical Limb Ischemia in Thrombospondin-1-Deficient Mice. PLoS One. 2008;3(12):e3950.

5. Committee to Review Dietary Reference Intakes for Vitamin D and Calcium, Food and Nutrition Board, Institute of Medicine. Dietary Reference Intakes for Calcium and Vitamin D. Washington, DC: National Academy Press. 2010.

6. Kudenchuk PJ, Maynard C, Martin JS, Wirkus M, Weaver WD. Comparison of presentation, treatment, and outcome of acute myocardial infarction in men versus women (the Myocardial Infarction Triage and Intervention Registry). Am J Cardiol. 1996;78:9–14.

7. Charney P, ed. Coronary artery disease in women: what all physicians need to know. Philadelphia: American College of Physicians. 1999.

8. Lesser M. Testosterone propionate therapy in one hundred cases of angina pectoris. J Clin Endocrinol. 1946;6:549-57.

9. Wu SZ, Weng XZ. Therapeutic effects of an androgenic preparation on myocardial ischemia and cardiac function in 62 elderly male coronary heart disease patients. Chin Med J (Engl). 1993;106:415-8.

10. Phillips GB, Pinkernell BH, Jing TY. The association of hypotestosteronemia with coronary artery disease in men. Arterioscler Thromb. 1994;14:701-6.

11. Winkler U. Effects of androgens on haemostasis. Maturitas. 1996;24:147-55.

12. Iellamo F, Volterrani M, Caminiti G, Karam R, Massaro R, Fini M, et al. Testosterone therapy in women with chronic heart failure: a pilot double-blind, randomized, placebo-controlled study. J Am Coll Cardiol. 2010 Oct 12;56(16):1310-6.

13. Stephens N, Parsons A, Schofield P, Kelly F, Cheeseman K, Mitchinson MJ. Randomised controlled trial of vitamin E in patients with coronary disease: Cambridge Heart Antioxidant Study (CHAOS). The Lancet. 1996;347:781-6.

14. Axford-Gately R, Wilson G. Myocardial infarct size reduction by single high doses or repeated low dose vitamin E supplementation in rabbits. Can J Cardiol. 1993;9:94-8.

15. DeMaio S, King Sd, Lembo N, Roubin GS, Hearn JA, Bhagavan HN, et al. Vitamin E supplementation, plasma lipids and incidence of restenosis after percutaneous transluminal coronary angioplasty (PCTA). J Am Coll Nutr. 1992;11:68-73.

16. Rapola J, Virtamo J, Haukka J, Heinonen OP, Albanes D, Taylor PR, et al. Effect of vitamin E and beta carotene on the incidence of angina pectoris. JAMA. 1996;275:693-8.

17. Steiner M. Influence of vitamin E on platelet function in humans. J Am Coll Nutr. 1991;10:466-73.

18. Enstrom JE, Kanim LE, Klein MA. Vitamin C intake and mortality among a sample of the United States population. Epidemiology. 1992;3:194-202.

19. McCully K. The Homocysteine Revolution. Keats Publishing, Inc. 1997.

20. McCully K. Homocysteine, folate, vitamin B6, and cardiovascular disease (editorial). JAMA. 1998;279:392-3.

21. Verhoef P, Hennekens CH, Malinow MR, Kok FJ, Willett WC, Stampfer MJ. A prospective study of plasma homocyst(e)ine and risk of myocardial infarction in US physicians. JAMA. 1992;268:877-81.

22. Stampfer M, Malinow M. Can lowering homocysteine levels reduce cardiovascular risk? N Engl J Med. 1995;332:328-9.

23. Bélanger A, Candas B, Dupont A, Cusan L, Diamond P, Gomez JL, et al. Changes in serum concentrations of conjugated and unconjugated steroids in 40- to 80-year-old men. J Clin Endocrinol Metab. 1994 Oct;79(4):1086-90.

24. Labrie F, Bélanger A, Cusan L, Gomez JL, Candas B. Marked decline in serum concentrations of adrenal C19 sex steroid precursors and conjugated androgen metabolites during aging. J Clin Endocrinol Metab. 1997 Aug;82(8):2396-402.

25. Regelson W, Colman C. The Superhormone Promise. New York, Simon & Schuster. 1996.

26. Salom MG, Jabaloyas JM. [Testosterone deficit syndrome and erectile dysfunction]. Arch Esp Urol. 2010 Oct;63(8):663-70.

27. Nikoobakht M, Pourkasmaee M, Nasseh H. The relationship between lipid profile and erectile dysfunction. Urol J. 2005 Winter;2(1):40-4.

28. Vrentzos GE, Paraskevas KI, Mikhailidis DP. Dyslipidemia as a risk factor for erectile dysfunction. Curr Med Chem. 2007;14(16):1765-70.

29. Padrón RS, Más J, Zamora R, Riverol F, Licea M, Mallea L, et al. Lipids and testicular function. Int Urol Nephrol. 1989;21(5):515-9.

30. Rizvi K, Hampson JP, Harvey JN. Do lipid-lowering drugs cause erectile dysfunction? A systematic review. Fam Pract. 2002 Feb;19(1):95-8.

31. Carvajal A, Macias D, Sáinz M, Ortega S, Martín Arias LH, Velasco A, et al. HMG CoA reductase inhibitors and impotence: two case series from the Spanish and French drug monitoring systems. Drug Saf. 2006;29(2):143-9.

32. Morgentaler A, Bruning CO 3rd, DeWolf WC. Occult prostate cancer in men with low serum testosterone levels. JAMA. 1996 Dec 18;276(23):1904-6.

33. Schatzl G, Madersbacher S, Haitel A, Gsur A, Preyer M, Haidinger G, et al. Associations of serum testosterone with microvessel density, androgen receptor density and androgen receptor gene polymorphism in prostate cancer. J Urol. 2003 Apr;169(4):1312-5.

34. Vatten LJ, Ursin G, Ross RK, Stanczyk FZ, Lobo RA, Harvei S, et al. Androgens in serum and the risk of prostate cancer: a nested case-control study from the Janus serum bank in Norway. Cancer Epidemiol Biomarkers Prev. 1997 Nov;6(11):967-9.

35. Chodak GW, Vogelzang NJ, Caplan RJ, Soloway M, Smith JA. Independent prognostic factors in patients with metastatic (stage D2)

prostate cancer. The Zoladex Study Group. JAMA. 1991 Feb 6;265(5):618-21.

36. MacGregor, EA. Prevention and treatment of menstrual migraine. Drugs. 2010;70(14):1799–818.

37. Lay CL, Broner SW. Migraine in women. Neurol Clin. 2009 May;27(2):503-11.

38. Stovner LJ, Zwart JA, Hagen K, Terwindt GM, Pascual J. Epidemiology of headache in Europe. Eur J Neurol. 2006 Apr;13(4):333-45.

39. Bartels EM, Dreyer L, Jacobsen S, Jespersen A, Bliddal H, Danneskiold-Samsøe B. [Fibromyalgia, diagnosis and prevalence. Are gender differences explainable?]. Ugeskr Laeger. 2009;171(49):3588–92.

40. Olin R. Fibromyalgia. A neuro-immuno-endocrinologic syndrome? Lakartidningen. 1995 Feb 22;92(8):755-8.

41. Schochat T, Beckmann C. Sociodemographic characteristics, risk factors and reproductive history in subjects with fibromyalgia—results of a population-based case-control study. Z Rheumatol. 2003;62(1):46-59.

42. Adler GK, Manfredsdottir VF, Creskoff KW. Neuroendocrine abnormalities in fibromyalgia. Curr Pain Headache Rep. 2002 Aug;6(4):289-98.

43. Hudson JI, Goldenberg DL, Pope HG Jr, Keck PE Jr, Schlesinger L. Comorbidity of fibromyalgia with medical and psychiatric disorders. Am J Med. 1992 Apr;92(4):363-7.

44. Matsumoto Y. Fibromyalgia syndrome. Nippon Rinsho. 1999 Feb;57(2):364-9.

45. Russo EB. Clinical endocannabinoid deficiency (CECD): can this concept explain therapeutic benefits of cannabis in migraine, fibromyalgia, irritable bowel syndrome and other treatment-resistant conditions? Neuro Endocrinol Lett. 2004 Feb-Apr;25(1-2):31-9.

46. Nicolodi M, Sicuteri F. Fibromyalgia and migraine, two faces of the same mechanism. Serotonin as the common clue for pathogenesis and therapy. Adv Exp Med Biol. 1996;398:373-9.

47. Thompson D, Lettich L, Takeshita J. Fibromyalgia: an overview. Curr Psychiatry Rep. 2003 Jul;5(3):211-7.

48. Pongratz D, Spath M. Fibromyalgia. Fortschr Neurol Psychiatr. 2001 Apr;69(4):189-93.

49. Hug C, Gerber NJ. Fibromyalgia syndrome, a frequently misdiagnosed entity. Schweiz Med Wochenschr. 1990 Mar 24;120(12):395-401.

50. Moldofsky H. Management of sleep disorders in fibromyalgia. Rheum Dis Clin North Am. 2002 May;28(2):353-65.

51. Rohr UD, Herold J. Melatonin deficiencies in women. Maturitas. 2002 Apr 15;41 Suppl 1:S85-104.

52. Available at: http://arthritis.about.com/od/rheumatoidarthritis/a/rheumatoidlung.htm. Accessed April 22, 2012.

53. de Groot K. [Renal manifestations in rheumatic diseases]. Internist (Berl). 2007;48(8):779–85.

54. Wolfe F, Mitchell DM, Sibley JT, Fries JF, Bloch DA, Williams CA, et al. The mortality of rheumatoid arthritis. Arthritis Rheum. 1994 Apr;37(4):481-94.

55. Aviña-Zubieta JA, Choi HK, Sadatsafavi M, Etminan M, Esdaile JM, Lacaille D. "Risk of cardiovascular mortality in patients with rheumatoid arthritis: a meta-analysis of observational studies". Arthritis Rheum. 2008 Dec 15;59(12):1690-7.

56. Baecklund E, Iliadou A, Askling J, Ekbom A, Backlin C, Granath F, et al. Association of chronic inflammation, not its treatment, with increased lymphoma risk in rheumatoid arthritis. Arthritis Rheum. 2006 Mar;54(3):692-701.

57. Franklin J, Lunt M, Bunn D, Symmons D, Silman, A. Incidence of lymphoma in a large primary care derived cohort of cases of inflammatory polyarthritis. Ann Rheum Dis. 2006 May;65(5):617-22.

58. Available at: http://www.nice.org.uk/nicemedia/pdf/CG059FullGuideline.pdf. Accessed April 22, 2012.

59. Centers for Disease Control and Prevention (CDC) (February 2001). Prevalence of disabilities and associated health conditions among adults—United States, 1999. MMWR Morb Mortal Wkly Rep. 50(7):120–5.

60. Kolf CM, Cho E, Tuan RS. Mesenchymal stromal cells. Biology of adult mesenchymal stem cells: regulation of niche, selfrenewal and differentiation. Arthritis Res Ther. 2007;9:204.

61. Phinney DG, Prockop DJ. Concise review: mesenchymal stem/ multipotent stromal cells: the state of transdifferentiation and modes of tissue repair—current views. Stem Cells. 2007;25:2896–902.

62. Satija NK, Gurudutta GU, Sharma S, Afrin F, Gupta P, Verma YK, et al. Mesenchymal stem cells: molecular targets for tissue engineering. Stem Cells Dev. 2007;16:7–23.

63. Suzuki M, Wright LS, Marwah P, Lardy HA, Svendsen CN. Mitotic and neurogenic effects of dehydroepiandrosterone (DHEA) on human neural stem cell cultures derived from the fetal cortex. Proc Natl Acad Sci U S A. 2004 Mar 2;101(9):3202-7.

64. Pinnock SB, Lazic SE, Wong HT, Wong IH, Herbert J. Synergistic effects of dehydroepiandrosterone and fluoxetine on proliferation of progenitor cells in the dentate gyrus of the adult male rat. Neuroscience. 2009 Feb 18;158(4):1644-51.

65. Han K, Lee JE, Kwon SJ, Park SY, Shim SH, Kim H, et al. Human amnion-derived mesenchymal stem cells are a potential source for uterine stem cell therapy. Cell Prolif. 2008 Oct;41(5):709-25.

66. Labombarda F, González SL, Lima A, Roig P, Guennoun R, Schumacher M, et al. Effects of progesterone on oligodendrocyte progenitors, oligodendrocyte transcription factors, and myelin proteins following spinal cord injury. Glia. 2009 Jun;57(8):884-97.

67. De Nicola AF, Gonzalez SL, Labombarda F, Deniselle MC, Garay L, Guennoun R, et al. Progesterone treatment of spinal cord injury: Effects on receptors, neurotrophins, and myelination. J Mol Neurosci. 2006;28(1):3-15.

68. Labombarda F, Gonzalez S, Gonzalez Deniselle MC, Garay L, Guennoun R, Chumacher M, et al. Progesterone increases the expression of myelin basic protein and the number of cells showing NG2 immunostaining in the lesioned spinal cord. J Neurotrauma. 2006 Feb;23(2):181-92.

69. Foresta C, Caretta N, Lana A, De Toni L, Biagioli A, Ferlin A, et al. Reduced number of circulating endothelial progenitor cells in hypogonadal men. J Clin Endocrinol Metab. 2006 Nov;91(11):4599-602.

70. Siiteri P, Wilson JD. Testosterone formation and metabolism during male sexual differentiation in the human embryo. J Clin Endocrinol Metab. 1974;38:113.

71. Golomb BA, Stattin H, Mednick S. Low cholesterol and violent crime. J Psychiatr Res. 2000 Jul-Oct;34(4-5):301-9.

72. Atmaca M, Kuloglu M, Tezcan E, Ustundag B, Bayik Y. Serum leptin and cholesterol levels in patients with bipolar disorder. Neuropsychobiology. 2002;46(4):176-9.

73. Cassidy F, Carroll BJ. Hypocholesterolemia during mixed manic episodes. Eur Arch Psychiatry Clin Neurosci. 2002 Jun;252(3):110-4.

74. Fukui M, Soh J, Tanaka M, Kitagawa Y, Hasegawa G, Yoshikawa T. Low serum testosterone concentration in middle-aged men with type 2 diabetes. Endocr J. 2007;54:871–7.

75. Grossman M, Thomas MC, Panagiotopoulos S, Sharpe K, Macisaac RJ, Clark S, et al. Low testosterone levels are common and associated with insulin resistance in men with diabetes. J Clin Endocrinol Metab. 2008;93(5):1834–40.

76. Haffner SM, Shaten J, Stern MP, Smith GD, Kuller L. Low levels of sex hormone-binding globulin and testosterone predict the development of non-insulin-dependent diabetes mellitus in men. MRFIT Research Group. Multiple Risk Factor Intervention Trial. Am J Epidemiol. 1996;143:889–97.

77. Kapoor D, Goodwin E, Channer KS, Jones TH. Testosterone replacement therapy improves insulin resistance, glycaemic control, visceral adiposity and hypercholesterolaemia in hypogonadal men with type 2 diabetes. Eur J Endocrinol. 2006;154:899–906.

78. Picard F, Wanatabe M, Schoonjans K, Lydon J, O'Malley BW, Auwerx J. Progesterone receptor knockout mice have an improved glucose homeostasis secondary to beta -cell proliferation. Proc Natl Acad Sci U S A. 2002 Nov 26;99(24):15644-8.

Part VII

1. Available at: http://www.iaso.org/iotf/obesity/. Accessed April 22, 2012.

2. Vertuani S, Angusti A, Manfredini S. The antioxidants and pro-antioxidants network: an overview. Curr Pharm Des. 2004;10(14):1677-94.

3. Futoryan T, Gilchrest BE. Retinoids and the skin. Nutr Rev. 1994;52:299-310.

4. Ross AC. Vitamin A and retinoids. In: Modern Nutrition in Health and Disease. 9th Edition (edited by Shils ME, Olson J, Shike M, Ross AC). Lippincott Williams and Wilkins, New York. 1999;305-27.

5. Ross AC, Stephensen CB. Vitamin A and retinoids in antiviral responses. FASEB J. 1996;10:979-85.

6. Semba RD. The role of vitamin A and related retinoids in immune function. Nutr Rev. 1998;56:S38-48.

7. Ross DA. Vitamin A and public health: Challenges for the next decade. Proc Nutr Soc. 1998;57:159-65.

8. Harbige LS. Nutrition and immunity with emphasis on infection and autoimmune disease. Nutr Health. 1996;10:285-312.

9. Sommer A. Nutritional Blindness: Xeropthalmia and Keratomalacia. Oxford University Press, London and New York. 1982.

10. Ross AC. Vitamin A status: Relationship to immunity and the antibody. Proc Soc Exp Biol Med. 1992;200:303-20.

11. Stephens D, Jackson PL, Gutierrez Y. Subclinical vitamin A deficiency: A potentially unrecognized problem in the United States. Pediatr Nurs. 1996;22:377-89.

12. Butler JC, Havens PL, Sowell AL, Huff DL, Peterson DE, Day SE, et al. Measles severity and serum retinol (vitamin A) concentration among children in the United States. Pediatrics. 1993;91:1176-81.

13. Herbert V. Vitamin B12 in Present Knowledge in Nutrition. 17th ed. Washington, DC: International Life Sciences Institute Press. 1996.

14. Herbert V, Das K. Vitamin B12 in Modern Nutrition in Health and Disease. 8th ed. Baltimore, MD: Williams & Wilkins. 1994.

15. Zittoun J, Zittoun R. Modern clinical testing strategies in cobalamin and folate deficiency. Sem Hematol. 1999;36:35-46.

16. Combs G. Vitamin B12 in The Vitamins. New York: Academic Press, Inc. 1992.

17. Institute of Medicine. Food and Nutrition Board. Dietary Reference Intakes: Thiamin, Riboflavin, Niacin, Vitamin B6, Folate, Vitamin B12, Pantothenic Acid, Biotin, and Choline. Washington, DC: National Academy Press. 1998.

18. Mackey A, Davis S, Gregory J. Vitamin B6. In: Shils M, Shike M, Ross A, Caballero B, Cousins R, eds. Modern Nutrition in Health and Disease. 10th ed. Baltimore, MD: Lippincott Williams & Wilkins. 2005.

19. Kamen B. Folate and antifolate pharmacology. Semin Oncol. 1997;24:S18-30-S18-39.

20. Bottiglieri T. Folate, vitamin B12, and neuropsychiatric disorders. Nutr Rev. 1996;54:382-90.

21. McCormick D. Vitamin B6. In: Bowman B, Russell R, eds. Present Knowledge in Nutrition. 9th ed. Washington, DC: International Life Sciences Institute. 2006.

22. Jennings E. Folic acid as a cancer preventing agent. Med Hypothesis. 1995;45:297-303.

23. Freudenheim JL, Grahm S, Marshall JR, Haughey BP, Cholewinski S, Wilkinson G. Folate intake and carcinogenesis of the colon and rectum. Int J Epidemiol. 1991;20:368-74.

24. Giovannucci E, Stampfer MJ, Colditz GA, Hunter DJ, Fuchs C, Rosner BA, et al. Multivitamin use, folate, and colon cancer in women in the Nurses' Health Study. Ann Intern Med. 1998;129:517-24.

25. Jacob RA, Sotoudeh G. Vitamin C function and status in chronic disease. Nutr Clin Care. 2002;5:66-74.

26. Frei B, England L, Ames BN. Ascorbate is an outstanding antioxidant in human blood plasma. Proc Natl Acad Sci U S A. 1989;86:6377-81.

27. Carr AC, Frei B. Toward a new recommended dietary allowance for vitamin C based on antioxidant and health effects in humans. Am J Clin Nutr. 1999;69:1086-107.

28. Li Y, Schellhorn HE. New developments and novel therapeutic perspectives for vitamin C. J Nutr. 2007;137:2171-84.

29. Johnston CS, Martin LJ, Cai X. Antihistamine effect of supplemental ascorbic acid and neutrophil chemotaxis. Am Coll Nutr. 1992;11(2):172-6.

30. Clemetson. Histamine and ascorbic acid in human blood. J Nutr. 1980;4(4):662–8.

31. Johnston CS, Solomon RE, Corte C. Vitamin C depletion is associated with alterations in blood histamine and plasma free carnitine in adults. J Am Coll Nutr. 1996;15(6):586–91.

32. Wang AH, Still C. Old world meets modern: a case report of scurvy. Nutr Clin Pract. 2007;22:445-8.

33. Institute of Medicine. Food and Nutrition Board. Dietary Reference Intakes for Vitamin C, Vitamin E, Selenium, and Carotenoids. Washington, DC: National Academy Press. 2000.

34. Francescone MA, Levitt J. Scurvy masquerading as leukocytoclastic vasculitis: a case report and review of the literature. Cutis. 2005;76:261-6.

35. Weinstein M, Babyn P, Zlotkin S. An orange a day keeps the doctor away: scurvy in the year 2000. Pediatrics. 2001;108:E55.

36. Stephen R, Utecht T. Scurvy identified in the emergency department: a case report. J Emerg Med. 2001;21:235-7.

37. Bell EF. History of vitamin E in infant nutrition. Am J Clin Nutr. 1987 Jul;46(1 Suppl):183-6.

38. Traber MG. Vitamin E. In: Shils ME, Shike M, Ross AC, Caballero B, Cousins R, eds. Modern Nutrition in Health and Disease. 10th ed. Baltimore, MD: Lippincott Williams & Wilkins. 2006;396-411.

39. Sokol RJ, Kayden HJ, Bettis DB, Traber MG, Neville H, Ringel S, et al. Isolated vitamin E deficiency in the absence of fat malabsorption—

familial and sporadic cases: Characterization and investigation of causes. J Lab Clin Med. 1988 May;111(5):548-59.

40. Laplante P, Vanasse M, Michaud J, Geoffroy G, Brochu P. A progressive neurological syndrome associated with an isolated vitamin E deficiency. Can J Neurol Sci. 1984;11,561-4.

41. Krendel DA, Gilchrest JM, Johnson AO, Bossen EH. Isolated deficiency of vitamin E with progressive neurologic deterioration. Neurology. 1987 Mar;37(3):538-40.

42. Stumpf DA, Sokol R, Bettis D, Neville H, Ringel S, Angelini C, Bell R. Friedreich's disease: V. Variant form with vitamin E deficiency and normal fat absorption. Neurology. 1987;37(1):68-74.

43. Larnaout A, Belal S, Zouari M, Fki M, Ben Hamida C, Goebel, H, et al. Friedreich's ataxia with isolated vitamin E deficiency: a neuropathological study of a Tunisian patient. Acta Neuropathol. 1997 Jun;93(6):633-7.

44. Kohlschütter A, Hubner C, Jansen W, Lindner SG. A treatable familial neuromyopathy with vitamin E deficiency, normal absorption, and evidence of increased consumption of vitamin E. J Inherit Metab Dis. 1988;11 Suppl 2:149-52.

45. Burck U, Goebel HH, Kuhlendahl HD, Meier C, Goebel KM. Neuromyopathy and vitamin E deficiency in man. Neuropediatrics. 1981 Aug;12(3):267-78.

46. Traber MG, Sokol RJ, Ringel SP, Neville HE, Thellman CA, Kayden HJ. Lack of tocopherol in peripheral nerves of vitamin E-deficient patients with peripheral neuropathy. N Engl J Med. 1987 Jul 30;317(5):262-5.

47. Losowsky MS, Leonard PJ. Evidence of vitamin E deficiency in patients with malabsorption or alcoholism and the effects of therapy. Gut. 1967 Dec;8(6):539-43.

48. Farrell P, Bieri J, Fratantoni J, Wood R, Di Sant'Agnese, P. The occurrence and effects of human vitamin E deficiency. A study in patients with cystic fibrosis. J Clin Invest. 1977 Jul;60(1):233-41.

49. Institute of Medicine, Food and Nutrition Board. Dietary Reference Intakes for Calcium and Vitamin D. Washington, DC: National Academy Press. 2010.

50. Cranney C, Horsely T, O'Donnell S, Weiler H, Ooi D, Atkinson S, et al. Effectiveness and safety of vitamin D. Evidence Report/Technology Assessment No. 158 prepared by the University of Ottawa Evidence-based Practice Center under Contract No. 290-02.0021. AHRQ Publication No. 07-E013. Rockville, MD: Agency for Healthcare Research and Quality. 2007.

51. Holick MF. Vitamin D. In: Shils ME, Shike M, Ross AC, Caballero B, Cousins RJ, eds. Modern Nutrition in Health and Disease, 10th ed. Philadelphia: Lippincott Williams & Wilkins. 2006.

52. Norman AW, Henry HH. Vitamin D. In: Bowman BA, Russell RM, eds. Present Knowledge in Nutrition, 9th ed. Washington DC: ILSI Press. 2006.

Image Credits

Page 2 – The Anatomy Lesson of Dr. Nicholaes Tulp by Rembrandt van Rijin (1632)

Page 8, 23, 35, 38, 53, 61, 95, 98, 107, 136, 155, 186, 195 - by Daniel Owens, Vouch.

Page 13 – Vibro cholera under an electron microscope by Tom Kirn, Ron Taylor, Louisa Howard – Dartmouth Electron Microscope Facility (public domain)

Page 15 – Varicella virus by CDC Public Health Image Library (public domain)

Page 26 – Saint George and the Dragon by Gustave Moreau 1889-90

Page 50 – Heracles and the Hydra by Antonio Pollaiolo 1475

Page 76 – Dream of Aesculapius by Sebastiano Ricci, 1710

Page 112 – Prometheus by Gustave Moreau 1868

Page 150 – Angel of Death by Evelyn De Morgan 1890

Page 179 – Bacchus by Caravaggio 1595

Page 200 – Portrait de l'artiste sous les traits d'un moquer by Joseph Ducreux 1793

Index

About the Authors

Sergey A. Dzugan, MD, PhD

Dr. Dzugan is co-founder and Chief Scientific Officer of the Dzugan Institute of Restorative Medicine. Dr. Dzugan graduated from the Donetsk State Medical Institute (Ukraine) with a Doctorate of Medicine in 1979. After medical school, he performed his residency in general and cardiovascular surgery and became the Head of Heart Services in 1985. Dr. Dzugan has had a special training in vascular surgery, combustiology, microsurgery, arrhythmology, heart surgery, genetic testing, pedagogics and psychology. Dr. Dzugan was distinguished and highly trained educator, physician, and surgeon in the Ukraine.

In 1990, he received his PhD in Medical Science concerning heart rhythm disorder and subsequently became Assistant Professor at the Donetsk State Medical Institute. In May of 1991, he became the first Chief of the Department of cardiovascular Surgery and senior Heart Surgeon, in Donetsk District Regional Hospital, Ukraine.

In March of 1993, he became Associate Professor at Donetsk State Medical University. Dr. Dzugan performed a wide spectrum of operations for children and adults, including congenital and acquired heart diseases, and rhythm disorders. As the Head of Heart Surgery he had the highest medical skills and qualifications which can be awarded in his former country. As a practicing physician, Dr. Dzugan always found himself more in favor of holistic and natural medicines rather than synthetic. He always believed that strengthening one's immune system would do more to improve health than treating problems after they occur. Because of this, while performing heart surgeries, Dr. Dzugan became more interested in the preventive aspects of heart disease and began studying hormone treatments.

Dr. Dzugan moved to the United States from Ukraine in 1995 and in 1996, became a scientific consultant to Dr. Arnold Smith at the North Central Mississippi Regional Center in Greenwood, Mississippi. His role there was to stay current on the latest advances in nutraceutical treatments with a particular focus on such to improve immunity and the ability of patients to fight cancer. Dr. Dzugan has worked with the Cancer Center for more than 7 years and was a principle consultant of Anti-Aging strategy and biological therapy of cancer. The Cancer Center was active in clinical research and Dr. Dzugan's scholarly background as a clinical researcher helped proceed in a more organized and scientific fashion. In 1998, he has become board certified by the American Academy of Anti-Aging Medicine. His employer at the North Central Mississippi Regional Cancer Center has expressed stated that "Dr. Dzugan is extremely valuable to patient care and his role differentiates the North Central Mississippi Regional Cancer Center from that of any other centers in the states, because no other center has a full time well qualified staff person to meet the same function." Dr. Smith believes that "Dr. Dzugan is a brilliant, gifted physician whose talents we believe would make a significant contribution to the nation."

In 2001, Dr. Dzugan suggested a new hypothesis of hypercholesterolemia and developed a new statin-free method of high cholesterol treatment. At the same time he also developed a unique multimodal program for migraine management.

In October 2003, he moved to Ft. Lauderdale, Florida, and became the Manager of the Advisory Department at the Life Extension Foundation. Later, he became President of Life Extension Scientific Information Inc. In August 2006, Dr. Dzugan left the Life Extensions Foundation to create a scientific organization that consults physicians to develop the program for their patients to optimize physiology.

Dr. Dzugan was accepted (June, 30 2006) to the International Academy of Creative Endeavors (Moscow, Russia) as a Corresponding Member of the Academy for the outstanding contribution to the development of new methods of hypercholesterolemia and migraine treatment. One year later Academy awarded Dr. Dzugan with the honorary title of Academician. In December 2007, Dr. Dzugan was rewarded with Honoree Medal by this Academy for the personal input into the acquisition of science, culture, physical betterment of nation and strengthening of friendship between nations. He performed presentations multiple times at the prestigious International Congress on Anti-Aging Medicine. The topics of his presentations were related to cholesterol disorders, migraine, physiology optimization, stem cell therapy, cancer, immuno- and hormonorestorative therapy.

Dr. Dzugan is the author of 151 publications in medical journals and these publications include surgical, oncological, academic and anti-aging topics. Also, several articles were published in health related magazines, such as Life Extension Magazine and The South African Journal of Natural Medicine. He is the author of "Migraine Cure", "Dzugan Method | Restorative Medicine", "Your Blood Doesn't Lie!" and "The Magic of Cholesterol Numbers" books and holder of 3 patents (all related to heart surgery). Dr. Dzugan is a Member of the

Editorial Board of the Neuroendocrinilogy Letters and a member of the Medical Advisory Board at Life Extension Magazine. He is co-founder and President of iPOMS (International Physiology Optimization Medical Society).

Dr. Dzugan's current primary interests are physiologic therapy for elevated cholesterol, migraine, fatigue, fibromyalgia, behavioral and hormonal disorders.

Konstantine S. Dzugan

Konstantine is a scientific advisor of the Dzugan Institute of Restorative Medicine. Konstantine graduated from Florida Atlantic University in 2010.

He is the author of 2 publications in medical journals and one book. His primary interests include the development of programs for the optimization of physiology, botanical wizardry via the creation of chlorophyll rich biomass, explorations of drowned coasts, collection of semi-precious stones, research of lost cultures, and writing out inadequate extended metaphors.

THE RESTORATION OF THE

HUMAN
BODY

[IN 7 PARTS]

For more information please visit us on the web:
www.DzLogic.com
or contact us at 866-225-4877.